ST. PETE EATS
A Cookbook

ST. PETE EATS
A Cookbook

A collection of St. Pete's favorite flavors, prepared with health in mind with **DEPUTY MAYOR DR. KANIKA TOMALIN**

Copyright © 2020

All rights reserved. No part of this cookbook may be reproduced or used in a public manner without the prior written permission of the copyright owner, except for the use of brief quotations and the development of recipes within this book.

Edited by Emily Carbone, Alexis Chamberlain, Jenna Rimensnyder,
James Howard, Dr. Kanika Tomalin and the City of St. Petersburg
Marketing Department
Front cover photo by Maria Flanagan
Back cover photo by James Ostrand Photography
Design and Layout by Joey Neill and Todd Bates

ISBN: 978-1-7349155-0-1

Printed by LSC Communications
Printed and bound in the United States of America

www.healthystpetefl.com

CONTENTS

Dedication 6
About Healthy St. Pete 7
Foreword by Mayor Rick Kriseman 11
Introduction 15

APPETIZERS

Everyday I'm Brusslin' 25
Szechuan Tuna & Bamboo Rice 26
Shrimp Spring Roll 29
Snapper Crudo 31
Seafood Ceviche 33
Dr. Kanika Tomalin's Chicken Salad 35

SOUPS, SALADS & SANDWICHES

Heirloom Watercress 43
Power Bowl 45
Mediterranean Tuna Salad 47
The Adventurer Fresh Grouper 49
Greens with a Kick 51
Mango & Jicama Salad 53
Best Dressed Catch 55
Nicoise Salad 57
Call Me Turkey 59
Vegetarian Chili 61
Brie Bardot Sandwich 63
Dr. Kanika Tomalin's Jicama Avocado Salad . . . 65
Green Apple Cucumber Salad 67
PC Kimchi 69
Southern Braised Callaloo Stew 71

ENTREES

Dapper Snapper 79
Mapo Tofu 81
Vegan Asparagus Risotto 83
Taste of Southern Italy 85
Fresco Fish 87
Tropical Tails 88
Veggie Lasagna 91
Pasta Arrabbiata 93
Dr. Kanika Tomalin's Classic Caprese with Chicken 95
Cauliflower Steak 97
Ropa Vieja 99
Buddha Bowl 100

COCKTAILS

Sugar-Free Sips 109
Matcha Made in Heaven 111
Thyme After Time 113
The Aviator 115
Strawberry Mint Julep Mocktail 117
Hemingway Daiquiri 119
San Saba Songbird 121
Hemp Day 123
Dr. Kanika Tomalin's Be Prepeared 125

Participating locations 128
Photo credits 128

DEDICATION

This book is dedicated to the spirit of our beloved city, sweet St. Pete—vibrant and inclusive, colorful and connected. The spirit of St. Pete stirs in the souls of all her citizens with insistence to be seen and heard on every scene… by every herd.

It is the common answer to every question of why we call her home. Its celebration is the reason for this book.

Creation and production of *St. Pete Eats: A Cookbook* started more than a year before the coronavirus crept into our city; more than a year before we'd see St. Pete's spirit tested in unprecedented ways. At the time, the bustling sounds, lively sights and amazing tastes of our landscape blazed high every day and night of the week, in every corner of our community. Delicious offerings from world-class restaurants sat at the top of the countless reasons to call St. Pete home—right next to murals and museums, live music and the best mom and pops. Our restaurants infuse this place with unmatched flavor and experiences that bring us all out of our homes and together.

Then our streets emptied and our doors closed. And we wondered about the right time to release this book of amazing contributions from our area's most talented chefs. For me, the answer was clear. There's no better time to celebrate our food scene and the geniuses who make it great than right now when they need us most. This book is a symbol of our community's shared belief that our favorites will be there, waiting on the other side of this challenge, armed with all the great flavor and experiences we've come to love. Because, like St. Pete's spirit, some doors may be closed, but all that makes St. Pete special has gone nowhere. It is still here, more alive than ever. This book is a salute to that spirit and the special role our small businesses play in this paradise of a place we call home.

We are going to print with this book in an unprecedented time, like none our city has ever seen—or hopefully will ever see again. Special thanks to all of the restaurant and bar owners and chefs who contributed to this book; all proceeds from the sharing of your unmatched talent will go to provide relief in this unmatched time. Every purchase will benefit the City of St. Petersburg's Fighting Chance Fund, an initiative designed to help small businesses that have been most adversely impacted by this public health crisis. We were forced to separate, St. Pete, but we're never apart. We help each other. It's who we are.

ABOUT HEALTHY ST. PETE

A healthier St. Pete is a vital priority for businesses, families, and community leaders.

Approximately 27% of adults in St. Pete report being physically inactive in the past 30 days and 33% report having high blood pressure. These indicators put residents, as well as future generations, at greater risk for developing chronic diseases such as heart disease and diabetes. Chronic diseases are among the most common, costly, and preventable of all health problems. Health problems such as these affect our community's quality of life, our productivity, and ultimately, our length of life.

Health conditions and health outcomes can improve when we work together. In our role as servant leaders, we bring important partners to the table to advance health in our city. Through Healthy St. Pete, we implement institutional change, build community capacity through education and partnership, and implement innovative projects to advance St. Pete's health and well-being.

Each year, Healthy St. Pete serves the community and engages with more than 10,000 St. Pete residents. In a given year, Healthy St. Pete partners with more than 80 community events, teaches 60 health and wellness lessons, hosts Fit Family Nights, and engages 2,000 children. The Community Resource Bus Program opened its doors for 12 weeks, providing 560 free health screenings for 2,500 residents. Summer BreakSpot at Dell Holmes Park provided 2,500 free meals, ensuring that families who need it most have a chance to eat healthy.

More than 500 community members participate in the annual Healthy St. Pete Fit City 5K and 1 Mile Run, a celebration of health and wellness. The Health360 program offers $4,410 in produce vouchers. Ninety-two percent of participants report an increase in their confidence to cook healthy foods and 66% report lower blood pressure and BMI. Fresh and Rec Stop finished the fiscal year selling 2,620 pieces of produce at six locations across the city.

The mission of Healthy St. Pete is to build a culture of health in our city by making the healthy choice the easy choice through a collaborative community effort, like this cookbook.

Foreword by Mayor Rick Kriseman

As mayor, I get asked a lot of tough questions. Perhaps one of the most difficult—and politically risky—to answer is "What's your favorite restaurant?" When you are mayor of a city like St. Pete, home to countless exciting restaurants and innovative chefs, that's an impossible question to answer.

As our city has evolved, so has our culinary scene. Not long ago, the best food options were concentrated along Beach Drive and sparsely populated throughout our downtown. Today, we enjoy acclaimed restaurants across our city. We are bursting with as much flavor as we are sunshine.

We're also more mindful than ever. We've joined with our restaurant community to ensure healthy options are available to everyone in our city. I am proud of the work our Healthy St. Pete team, led by Deputy Mayor and City Administrator Dr. Kanika Tomalin, has accomplished.

Creating a culture of health and making healthy choices is our mission and the purpose of this cookbook. To that end, we have engaged our restaurateurs, chefs, citizens and community partners to promote the health and well-being of our residents. And it's working.

I love good food, and I love doing my part as both a mayor and a resident to make St. Pete a fun foodie town. One of the great joys of being mayor is cutting the ribbon during a new restaurant opening, then coming back as a patron to enjoy a meal. A greater joy, however, is knowing that those who live, work and play in St. Pete can do so in a healthy manner.

I hope you enjoy this book and the delicious recipes that make St. Pete unique.

DR. KANIKA TOMALIN
Deputy Mayor and City Administrator

I know you think you just picked up a cookbook, but for me, it's much more a love story... an incredible mashup of three things I love most in this world: food, family and St. Pete! Combined, these three beloveds account for most of my time and passion. I'm excited to share this with you in this cookbook.

We're so fortunate to live in a city that overflows with flavor and epicurean experiences. It's my mission as St. Pete's Deputy Mayor and City Administrator to infuse those flavors with delicious, healthy options. There are a million wonderful reasons to call St. Pete home, and we want healthy living to shine as one of those reasons.

For me, food is all about love. From dreaming up a meal to preparing and enjoying it with family and friends—every step is a celebration. Food has played an invaluable role in my life. It keeps me connected to family, punctuates fun with friends, and teaches me something new every time I'm in the kitchen. Whether cooking an elaborate meal for others or serving a simple dish, cooking is an expression of love, creating memories that will last a lifetime.

My earliest memories unfold in a kitchen, surrounded by people I love. My mom was one of 15, and my grandma's house was always filled with aunts and uncles, cousins and family friends feasting on dishes my grandmother had lovingly prepared. Sometimes, it was a formal table filled with decadent Southern dishes, other times it was a simple lasagne sitting on the stove. Whatever the dish, every bite was cherished. Looking back, I believe the joy was more about the company than the meal, but the nostalgia of those flavors always brings me back to these special memories.

That love brought me to start a family of my own with my husband, Terry Tomalin. A great adventurer, who hailed from a family of nine, Terry filled our lives—and our table—with freshly-caught, perfectly-prepared meals. Some he created, some handed down from his family in Sicily. Terry did many things well, and cooking was one of them. A lifetime of exposure to exceptional food has taught me how to be a pretty good cook. I've learned to express love through food and to do so in ways that honor my family's health and my community's culinary landscape—sourcing ingredients locally, in ways that are sustainable.

As a fifth-generation resident of St. Pete, I've watched the city evolve into a welcoming haven of inclusivity that celebrates diversity and the value that it brings. We are rewriting our story, and food has become a central character in St. Pete's narrative.

We're blessed with a diverse food landscape that is illustrated with robust flavors that show our vast cultural connections. Food takes us across cultural lines in a comfortable, inviting way that leads to new exposure and experiences.

As St. Pete's next chapter unfolds, adventurous eaters will carry their culinary explorations beyond the

occasional evening out and into their own kitchens. All who appreciate the accessibility of fresh, locally-sourced ingredients prepared with love will contribute to our community's culinary excellence not only as consumers, but also as creators.

This book's mission is to give at-home cooks a taste of the flavors that can be found throughout the city—with a healthier spin. That's where our talented chef-driven restaurants, partnered with the Healthy St. Pete program, come into play.

Healthy St. Pete is a citywide community engagement and empowerment initiative that helps us eat, live, shop and play healthier.

I've shared some of my own favorite recipes, and have enlisted the expertise of some of St. Pete's finest chefs.

Ambassadors of Healthy St. Pete are the architects who have built our city's food scene into what it is today. From Central Avenue and South St. Pete to West Central Village and Beach Drive, these seasoned chefs have graciously shared gems from their culinary arsenals for readers to create and enjoy.

As you navigate this cookbook, feel the passion of chefs who are on the cutting edge of St. Pete's culinary scene, and let them guide you through each recipe.

These are the flavors we've grown to know and love, conceived by the chefs we all admire, created by you, and for you and your loved ones to enjoy at home. The only gift greater than being served a meal created with love, is to be the one creating with love. Enjoy!

"For me, food is all about love. From dreaming up a meal to preparing and enjoying it with family and friends—every step is a celebration."

- CHAPTER 1 -
APPETIZERS

Appetizers aren't solely meant for dinner parties. In fact, I've found that if there's not a healthy appetizer or light pre-dinner bite, my kids will raid the cabinets for junk food.

Appetizers can help you avoid ravenous teens, restless guests and set the tone for what's to come. Small, communal plates give guests an opportunity to connect and give you the time you need to put finishing touches on the main course. Our lineup of chefs have compiled a list of dishes that range from casual to elevated to help you fight the pre-dinner munchies, and arm you with some quick, and easy-to-serve deliciousness the next time you host.

25	EVERYDAY I'M BRUSSLIN'
26	SZECHUAN TUNA & BAMBOO RICE
29	SHRIMP SPRING ROLL
31	SNAPPER CRUDO
33	SEAFOOD CEVICHE
35	DR. KANIKA TOMALIN'S CHICKEN SALAD

SERVING SIZE 1

URBAN BREW AND BBQ

EVERYDAY I'M BRUSSLIN'
CHICKEN BREAST WITH CHARRED BRUSSEL SPROUTS

8 ounces brussels sprouts, rinsed and halved
Extra virgin olive oil
Salt and pepper
6 ounces boneless, skinless chicken breast
1 tsp pork rub (mixture of smoked paprika, brown sugar, chili powder, kosher salt and black pepper)
2 tsp bacon bits (optional)
2 tbsp peppercorn dressing

Urban Brew and BBQ is known for their creative ways of preparing brussels sprouts, and this healthy favorite will melt in your mouth. Fresh, tender roasted brussels sprouts cooked to perfection, topped with blackened chicken, a creamy peppercorn ranch dressing and crispy bacon bits are a crowd favorite.

1. In a large bowl, combine brussels sprouts, a drizzle of olive oil, salt, and pepper; toss.
2. Place brussels sprouts on flat top (or griddle) flat-side down.
3. Cook on flat top for about 4 minutes until the side facing the skillet is charred. Remove from pan and place into 7" skillet serving vessel.
4. Season the chicken breast on both sides with pork rub.
5. Cook the chicken breast on flat top, about four minutes on each side or until cooked through.
6. Lay chicken breast on top of brussels sprouts to rest.
7. Sprinkle with bacon bits.
8. Drizzle with peppercorn.
9. Serve.

SERVING SIZE 1

THE BIRCH & VINE

SZECHUAN TUNA & BAMBOO RICE
GLOBALLY-INSPIRED GLUTEN-FREE DISH

Lauded as one of the top restaurants in downtown St. Pete, **The Birch & Vine** at The Birchwood is led by top chefs in the Tampa Bay area. Their chefs' creativity and years of experience stand out in globally-inspired dishes. The Birch & Vine's approachable, yet inventive, dishes are often playful and always flavorful. Don't be afraid to get creative plating your components.

3 ounces of ahi tuna

BAMBOO RICE
8 cups toasted bamboo rice
2 cups coconut milk
6 green onions
6 kaffir leaves
2 tbsp ginger
7 cups stock of your choice
4 cups water

SZECHUAN SESAME ASH SPICE
½ lb. white sesame seeds
½ lb. black sesame seeds
½ lb. Szechuan peppercorns
2 tsp raw sugar
3 tbsp salt

PUFFED JASMINE RICE
3 cups jasmine rice

YUZU EMULSION
1 tbsp yuzu juice
1 jumbo egg yolk
2 tbsp water
2 grams garlic
¼ tsp salt
¼ tsp sugar
¼ cup olive oil

Bamboo Rice
1. Toast bamboo rice in the oven at 350 degrees for 4 minutes.
2. In a sauce pot, place coconut milk, green onions, kaffir leaves ginger, stock, and water and bring to a boil. Once the mixutre reaches boil, remove from heat and strain.
3. Mix bamboo rice and coconut milk together in a baking dish.
4. Set oven to 325 degrees and bake for 20 to 30 minutes until liquid has absorbed into rice. Once achieved, place on flat pan to cool evenly.

Szechuan Sesame Ash Spice
1. Separately toast Szechuan peppercorns, white sesame, and black sesame for 3 to 5 minutes each.
2. Keeping spices separated, place in a coffee/spice grinder to achieve powder-like spice form. Once all three have been processed, mix together by hand.
3. Set aside.

Puffed Jasmine Rice
1. Heat grapeseed oil to 430 degrees.
2. Drop 1 cup of rice at a time into heated oil.
3. Leave in for no longer than 6 seconds each, strain.
4. Repeat process, and let rice dry out on paper towel.
5. Save leftover oil.

Yuzu Emulsion

1. In a medium sauce pot bring the yuzu juice, garlic, water and sugar to a simmer.
2. Cool down rapidly in an ice bath until room temperature.
3. In a blender, emulsify yuzu mixture with egg yolks, evoo and salt.

SERVING SIZE 8

LA V

SHRIMP SPRING ROLL
FRESH INGREDIENTS WITH A POP OF MINT

- 2 ounces rice vermicelli
- 8 rice wrappers
- 8 large cooked shrimp, peeled, deveined and halved
- 16 pcs of mint leaves
- 3 ounces beansprout
- 2 leaves lettuce, chopped
- 3 ounces hoisin sauce
- 1 ounce peanut sauce
- 1 tsp sugar
- 1 ounce water

La V is known for serving up colorful dishes of Vietnamese-fusion. The concept prides itself on preparing meals as if they were for their family. These spring rolls are prepared with fresh ingredients and without the use of cooking oil. You can also substitute any ingredients, including the protein of your preference. Get creative!

1. Bring a medium saucepan of water to boil, cook rice vermicelli 7 to 10 minutes, or until al dente, and drain.
2. Fill a large bowl with warm water. Dip one wrapper into the hot water for 1 second to soften.
3. Lay wrapper flat. In a row across the center, place 2 shrimp halves, a handful of vermicelli, mint, beansprout, and lettuce, leaving about 2 inches uncovered on each side.
4. Fold uncovered sides inward, then tightly roll the wrapper, beginning at the end with the lettuce.
5. Repeat with remaining ingredients.
6. In a small pan, cook the hoisin sauce, peanut, sugar, water together, stir until dissolved.
7. Serve spring rolls with ramekins filled with dipping sauce.

SERVING SIZE 1

ROCOCO STEAK

SNAPPER CRUDO
WITH CUCUMBER VINAIGRETTE

CUCUMBER VINAIGRETTE
1 small cucumber
¼ cup extra virgin olive oil
2 tbsp red wine vinegar
1 tbsp plain yogurt
1 tsp dijon mustard
1 tsp grated horseradish
1 tsp sugar
½ tsp sea salt

SNAPPER CRUDO
4 ounces fresh local red snapper
5 pcs blood orange segments
2 tbsp red radish, shaved and julienned
2 tbsp fresh chives
4 ounces cucumber vinaigrette
1 tsp lemon juice
Pinch sea salt
Yellow frisee for garnish

Rococo Steak opened its doors in 2013 in the downtown St. Pete area—and has cultivated a reputation as an award-winning culinary destination in Tampa Bay. The extensive wine list at Rococo Steak has been recognized by Wine Spectator with the Best of Award of Excellence for six years straight. This healthy dish can be adjusted for any type of local fish.

Cucumber Vinaigrette
1. Peel cucumber and cut into rough chop.
2. Combine all ingredients except the olive oil into a blender and mix.
3. Slowly add olive oil to emulsify.
4. Set aside.

Snapper Crudo
1. Cut snapper into sashimi slices and segment blood orange.
2. On a round plate, gently pour cucumber vinaigrette in the center of the plate making a circle.
3. Add the snapper and blood orange segments.
4. Sprinkle the radishes and chives around.
5. In a small bowl, combine the frisee and lemon juice and a pinch of sea salt. Garnish on top of crudo.

SERVING SIZE 4

CEVICHE
SEAFOOD CEVICHE
LIGHT, BRIGHT BITES

- 3 ounces small shrimp, blanched
- 3 ounces calamari rings, blanched
- 2 ounces bay scallops
- 8 ounces white fish
- ¼ cup red bell pepper, diced
- ¼ cup green bell pepper, diced
- ¼ cup red onion, thin sliced
- ¼ cup roma tomato, diced
- ½ cup tomato juice
- ½ tbsp garlic, chopped
- ¼ cup cilantro, chopped
- 1 tbsp Spanish paprika
- ½ tsp cumin
- ½ cup fresh lime juice
- ¼ cup extra virgin olive oil
- 2 tsp sugar
- Fresh diced jalapenos or cayenne to taste
- Plantain chips for serving

A pioneer for tapas and sangria, **Ceviche**, features Barcelona-inspired small plates and cocktails with authentic live music, bringing the magic of the Iberian coast to the Tampa Bay area. Ceviche, a refreshing dish of seafood marinated in citrus juice, is perfect for summer. It's light, bright and it won't weigh you down in the heat. This recipe allows fresh seafood to be the star of the show.

1. Blanch shrimp and calamari in lightly salted water for 20 seconds and then shock in ice water to stop the cooking process.
2. Gather the rest of your seafood and cut into half-inch pieces.
3. Place all seafood in a stainless bowl.
4. Add paprika, cumin, fresh lime juice, olive oil, and sugar. Mix well and store in refrigerator until the rest of the components ready to assemble.
5. Slice and remove the seeds from your peppers and tomatoes. Dice into half inch pieces, add to the stainless bowl.
6. Add chopped cilantro, garlic, and tomato juice.
7. Combine all ingredients and season with salt and white pepper to taste and incorporate well.
8. Allow to marinate in refrigerator for a minimum of 1 hour. This will allow all of the flavors to come together and the citrus will have time to cook the seafood.
9. Add plantain chips for extra crunch and added texture.

SERVING SIZE 6

DR. KANIKA TOMALIN'S CHICKEN SALAD
WITH GREEK YOGURT ON ENDIVE

- 2 chicken breasts
- 2 tbsp olive oil
- Salt and pepper
- ½ cup plain Greek yogurt
- ¼ cup dried cranberries
- 2 tbsp crushed walnuts (optional)
- 4 to 5 stalks endive

It's all about the appetizers. When I'm hosting family or friends, having a great appetizer on hand always brings smiles to their faces. This appetizer, inspired by my dear friend Erin Aebel, is one of my favorites because it's easy, delicious and a perfect balance to almost anything that follows.

1. Coat the bottom of a medium-sized frying pan with light olive oil.
2. Season chicken with your favorite seasoning, or lightly season with salt and pepper.
3. Brown chicken over medium heat until both sides are cooked through and appear golden. Remove from heat. Cube and refrigerate the chicken for easy, pre-party prep later. (Chicken can be cooked in advance and stored until ready to serve.)
4. Cut chicken into bite-sized cubes.
5. Combine all ingredients in a medium bowl. Drizzle lightly with olive oil until desired consistency.
6. Salt and pepper to taste.
7. Separate endive leaves on serving plate.
8. Scoop a spoonful into each boat.

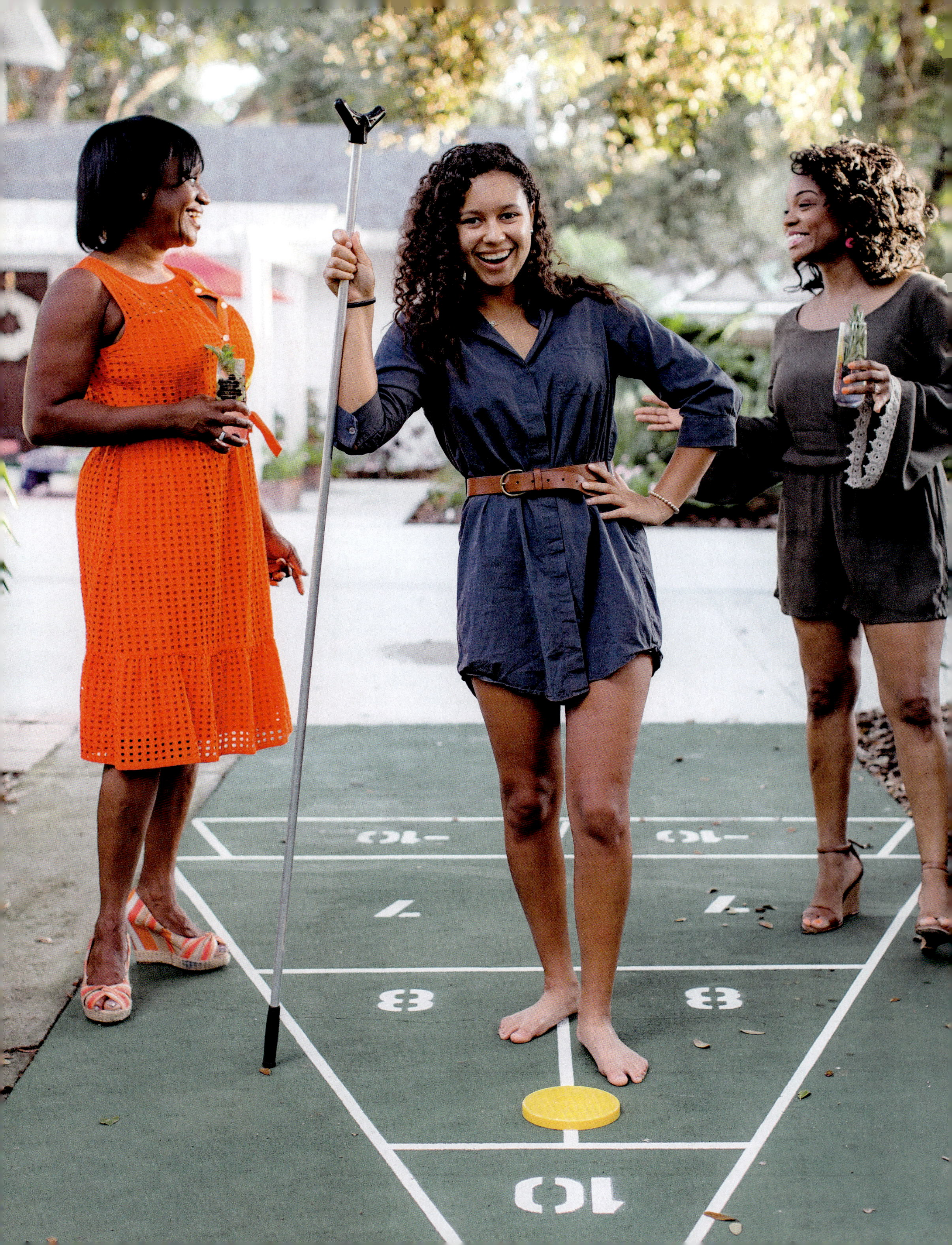

> *As a fifth-generation resident of St. Pete, I've watched the city evolve into a welcoming haven of inclusivity that celebrates diversity and the value that it brings. We are rewriting our story, and food has become a central character in St. Pete's narrative.*

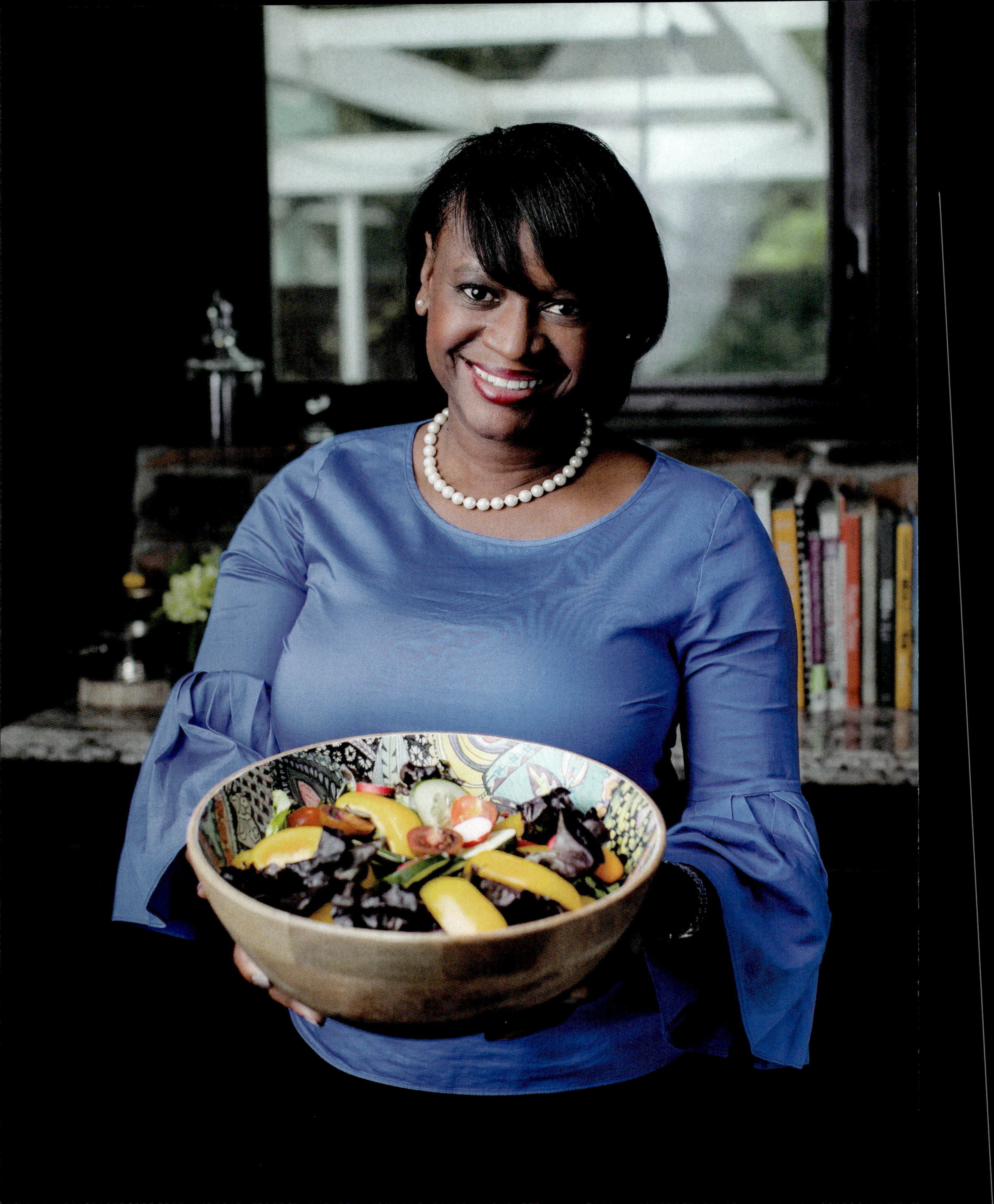

- CHAPTER 2 -
SOUPS, SALADS & SANDWICHES

Who says soups, salads and sandwiches are afterthoughts? Living in St. Pete means that there's no limit to our culinary experiences when it comes to any meal. As a mom, it's important for me to introduce my children to a wide variety of dishes, textures and flavors. These recipes are a great example of getting new flavors in front of my children while still serving them a delicious meal. Soups, salads and sandwiches can all be dressed up with vibrant vegetables, hearty proteins and filling grains to make everyone happy.

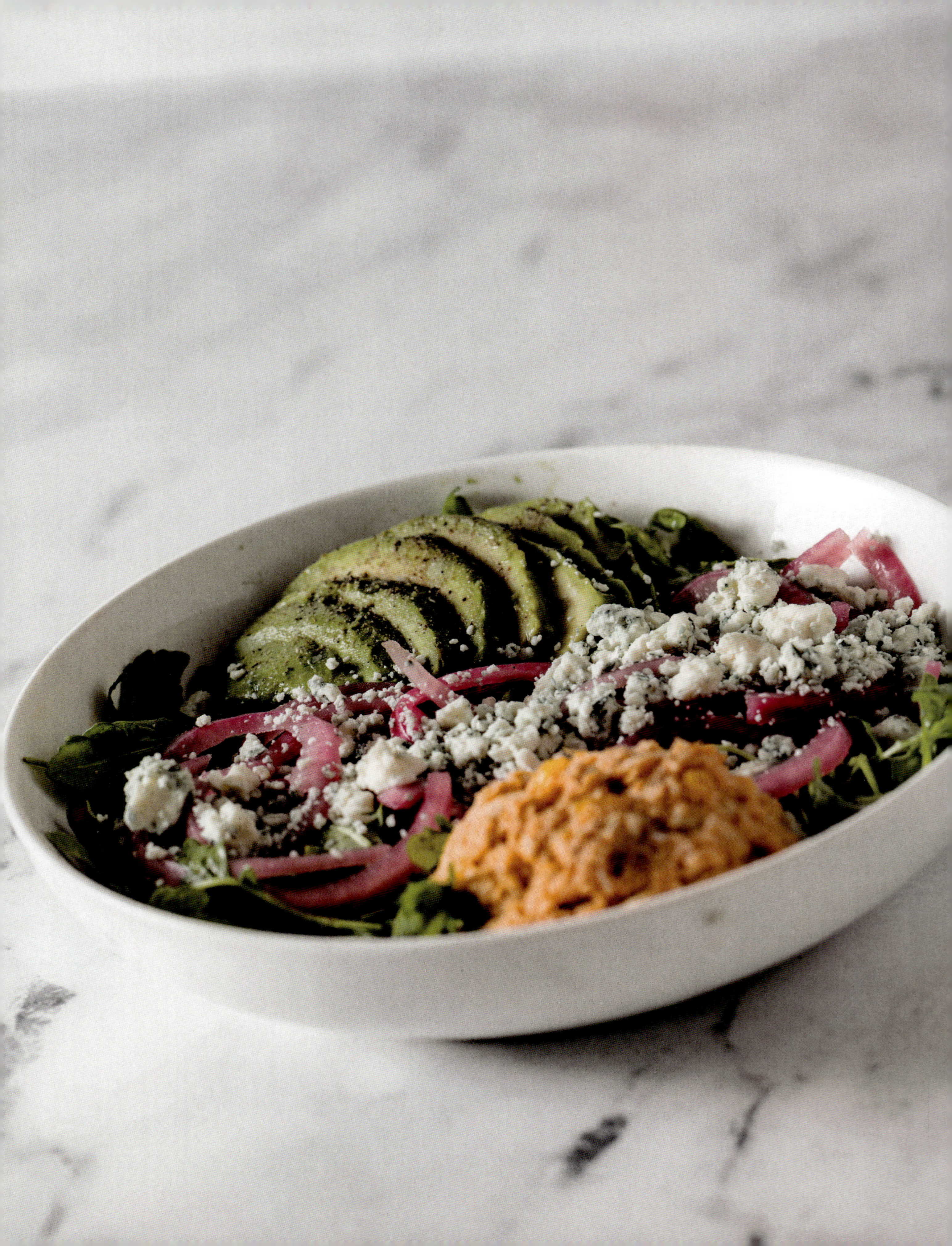

Page	Recipe
43	HEIRLOOM WATERCRESS
45	POWER BOWL
47	MEDITERRANEAN TUNA SALAD
49	THE ADVENTURER FRESH GROUPER
51	GREENS WITH A KICK
53	MANGO & JICAMA SALAD
54	BEST DRESSED CATCH
57	NICOISE SALAD
59	CALL ME TURKEY
61	VEGETARIAN CHILI
63	BRIE BARDOT SANDWICH
65	DR. KANIKA TOMALIN'S JICAMA AVOCADO SALAD
67	GREEN APPLE CUCUMBER SALAD
69	PC KIMCHI
71	SOUTHERN BRAISED CALLALOO STEW

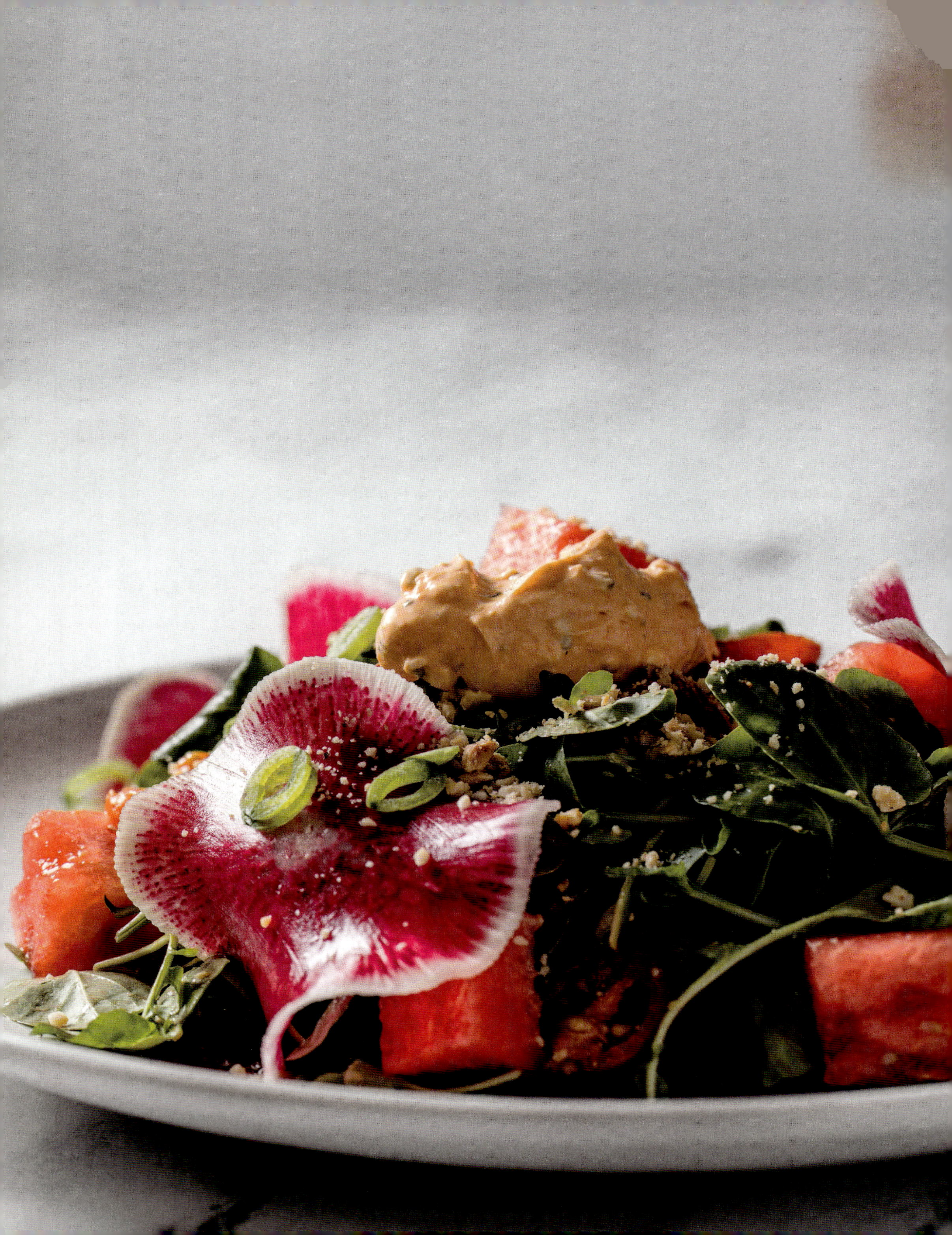

SERVING SIZE 1

THE MILL

HEIRLOOM WATERCRESS
HEARTY LEAFY SALAD WITH ROASTED HAZELNUTS

- 4 ounces heirloom watercress
- 2 ounces red beet jam
- 2 ounces snap peas
- 2 ounces diced watermelon
- 2 ounces dried cherry tomatoes
- 4 slices watermelon radish
- 1 ounce bacon salt roasted hazelnuts
- 2 ounces Honey Sambal goat cheese
- 2 ounces watermelon vinaigrette

The Mill restaurant is known for its rustic Americana fare with French and Southern influences. This heirloom watercress salad can be altered to your preference. Feel free to add your choice of protein or get creative with the toppings. All items can be substituted for the easiest to find at your grocery store.

1. Place beet jam on base of the plate.
2. Toss watercress with vinaigrette, then place on top of beet jam.
3. Place remaining ingredients on top of the salad to your preference.

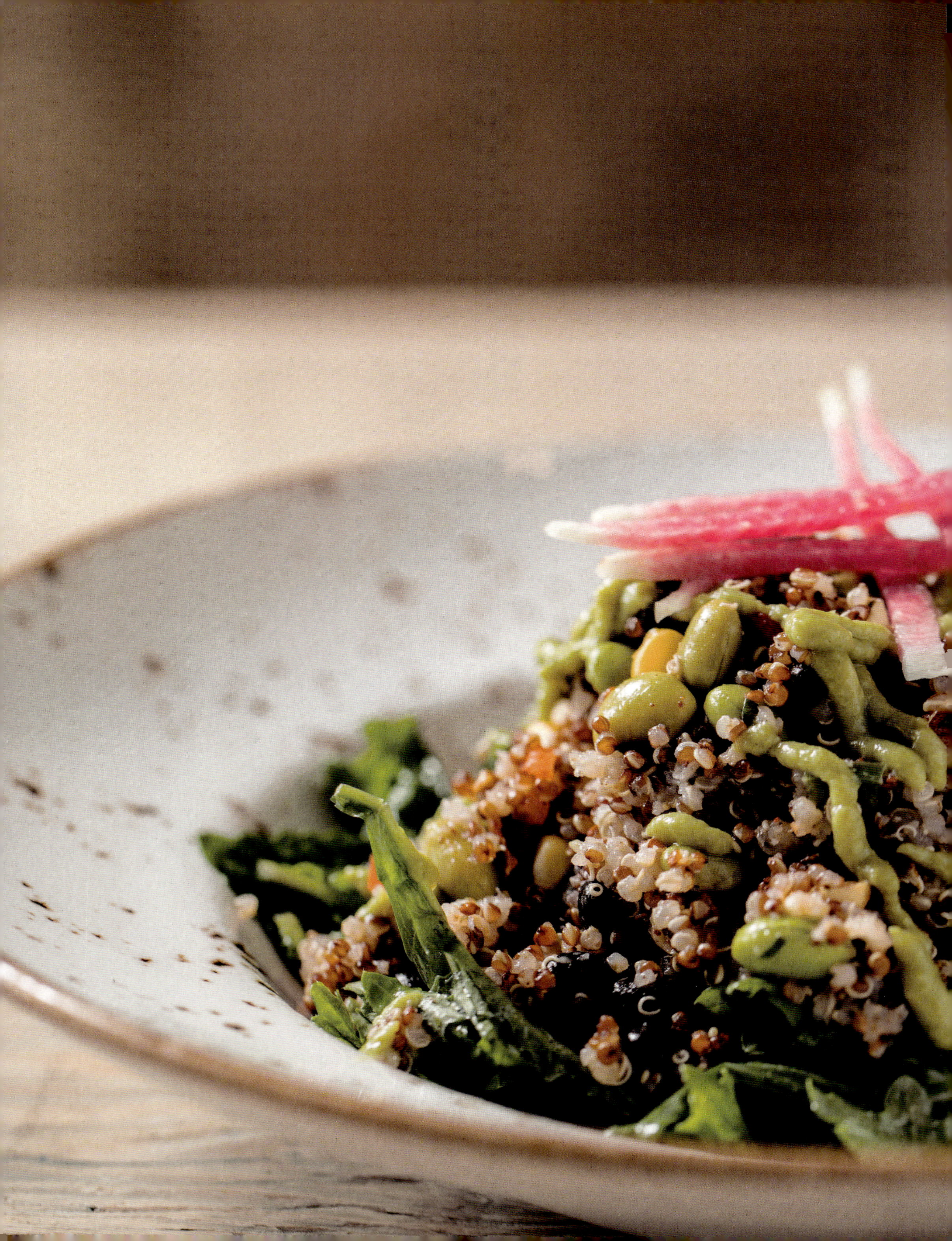

SERVING SIZE 4

PAUL'S LANDING
POWER BOWL
COLORFUL PROTEIN BOWL WITH SUPERFOOD QUINOA

Paul's Landing is an award-winning waterfront restaurant featuring local coastal provisions, live entertainment, great food and service with a cool vibe. This power bowl recipe is a great choice for vegans and vegetarians, or anyone looking for a healthy option. A protein of your choice can also easily be added to this dish.

BLACK BEAN AND CORN SALSA
1 can corn
1 can black beans
1 tomato, diced
½ cup shelled edamame
1 jalapeno, diced
1 bell pepper, diced
1 garlic clove, minced
Zest of 1 lime
2 tbsp cilantro, chopped
2 tsp chili powder
1 tsp cumin
Salt and pepper to taste

AVOCADO SAUCE
2 avocados
1 jalapeno, seeds removed
2 green onions, chopped
1 tbsp lime juice
2 tbsp cilantro, chopped
Salt and pepper to taste

CITRUS VINAIGRETTE
2 cups baby kale
1 cup cooked quinoa
1 tbsp lemon juice
1 tbsp lime juice
1 cup orange juice
2 tsp orange zest
Zest of one lime
2 tbsp honey
½ cup canola oil
Watermelon radish, for garnish (optional)

Black Bean and Corn Salsa
1. Combine all ingredients after preparation, season to taste.
2. Set aside.

Avocado Sauce
1. Combine all avocado sauce ingredients in blender.
2. Purée.
3. Set aside.

Citrus Vinaigrette
1. Combine all citrus vinaigrette in a small mixing bowl.
2. Whisk together and set aside until time to assemble. Make sure to whisk immediately before tossing.

Assembly
1. Cook 1 cup quinoa following package instructions.
2. Combine 2 cups black bean and corn salsa, 1 cup cooked quinoa, 2 cups baby kale, ¼ cup each of avocado sauce and citrus vinaigrette.
3. Gently toss.
4. Equally portion into 4 bowls.
5. If desired, garnish with protein of choice and sliced watermelon radish.

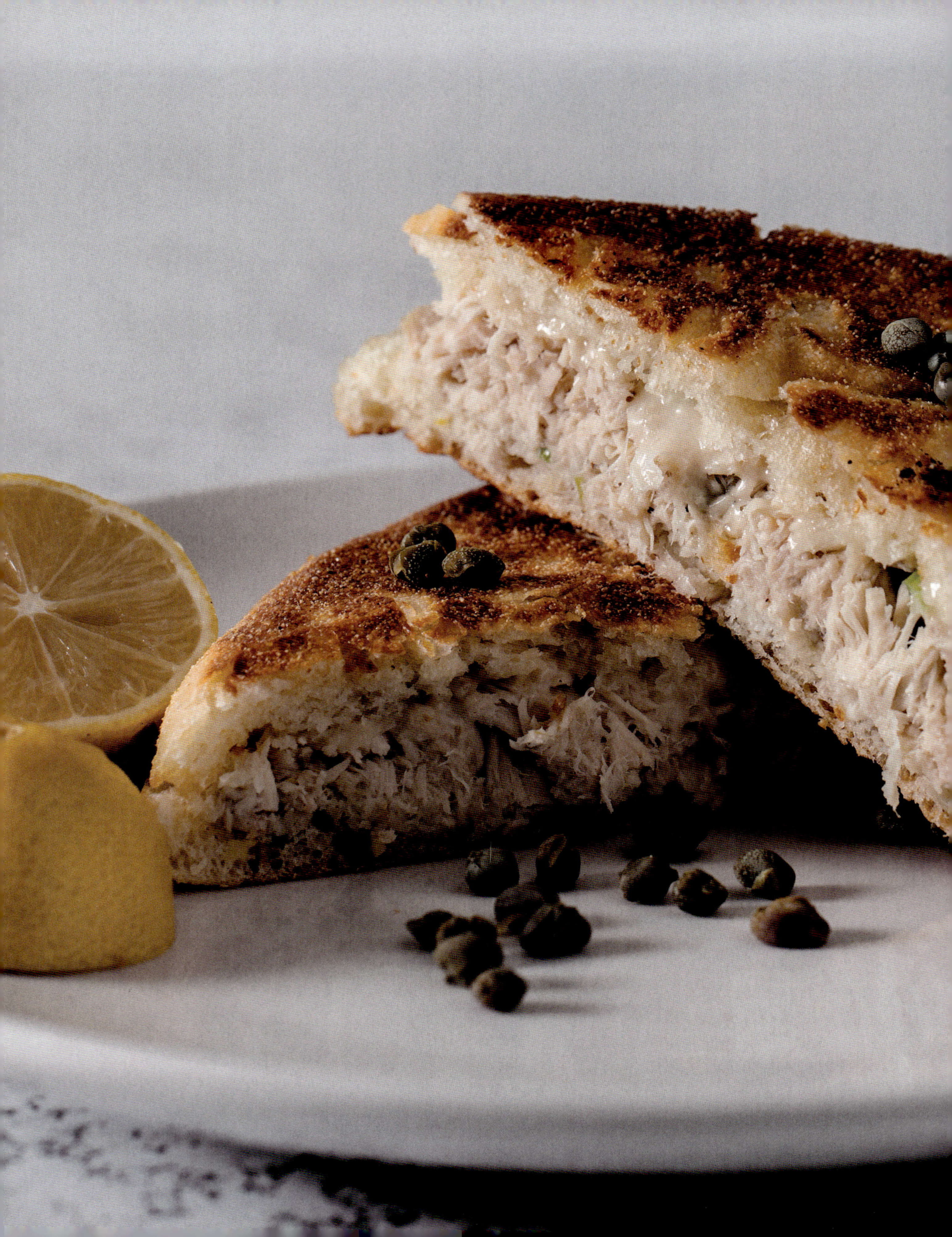

SERVING SIZE 2

BROOKLYN SOUTH

MEDITERRANEAN TUNA SALAD
WITH CAPERS AND BABY ARUGULA

- 2 cans Albacore tuna, drained
- ½ cup thinly sliced celery (including top leaves) or fresh fennel, depending on the season
- ½ cup packed small capers (non-pareil), drained
- Juice and zest of 2 lemons
- Drizzle of extra virgin olive oil, enough until mixture comes together
- Salt and pepper

Gourmet and specialty market, **Brooklyn South**, focuses on high-quality ingredients to make their artisanal cheeses and meats. Also known for their incredible sandwiches, Brooklyn South is a go-to neighborhood market in the Grand Central District. This tuna salad is a light and refreshing dish that can be enjoyed at anytime of the day. Replacing mayonnaise with freshly squeezed lemon juice and adding briny capers to the mix brightens up this classic.

1. Drain tuna and place in mixing bowl. Gently break up the bigger chunks with a fork.
2. Drain and lightly chop capers.
3. Combine tuna, capers, lemon zest, and juice into mixing bowl, gently mixing with large spoon.
4. Drizzle oil while mixing until incorporated and season with salt and pepper.
5. Scoop out onto a bed of baby arugula and shave approximately 1 to 2 ounces of Parmigiano-Reggiano over salad.

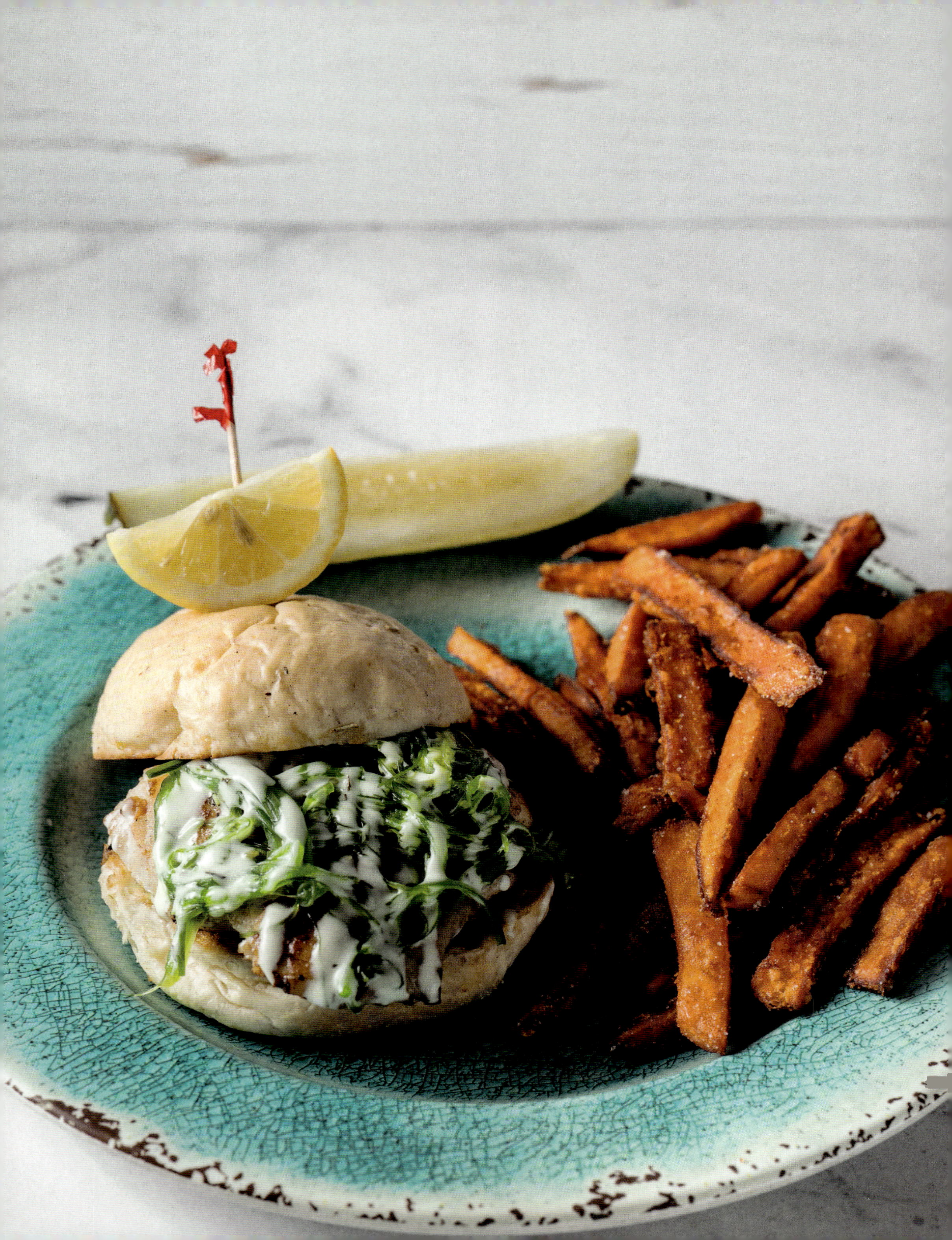

SERVING SIZE 1

THE TAVERN AT BAYBORO

THE ADVENTURER FRESH GROUPER
WITH CUCUMBER WASABI DRESSING

5 ounces fresh grouper
½ tsp Montreal seasoning
1 tbsp seaweed salad
2 tsp cucumber wasabi
1 roll or bun, halved
2 tbsp butter

The Tavern at Bayboro is a local hangout featuring delicious bites and local craft beers. The famous Original Crunchy Grouper Sandwich with fresh, locally-caught grouper is a must when you visit. It was renamed The Adventurer in 2016 after my late husband, Terry Tomalin, who was a great adventurer, known to enjoy this dayboat fresh catch after being out on the water.

1. Sprinkle Montreal seasoning on the non-skin side of the grouper.
2. Butter both sides of roll or bun, lay cut side down on pan to toast.
3. Place the fish on the grill or pan, skin side up, cooking for 2 to 3 minutes, then flip and cook for 2 to 3 minutes until cooked to preference.
4. Remove from heat and place on a grilled, buttered bun.
5. Top the fish with the seaweed salad and cucumber wasabi dressing.

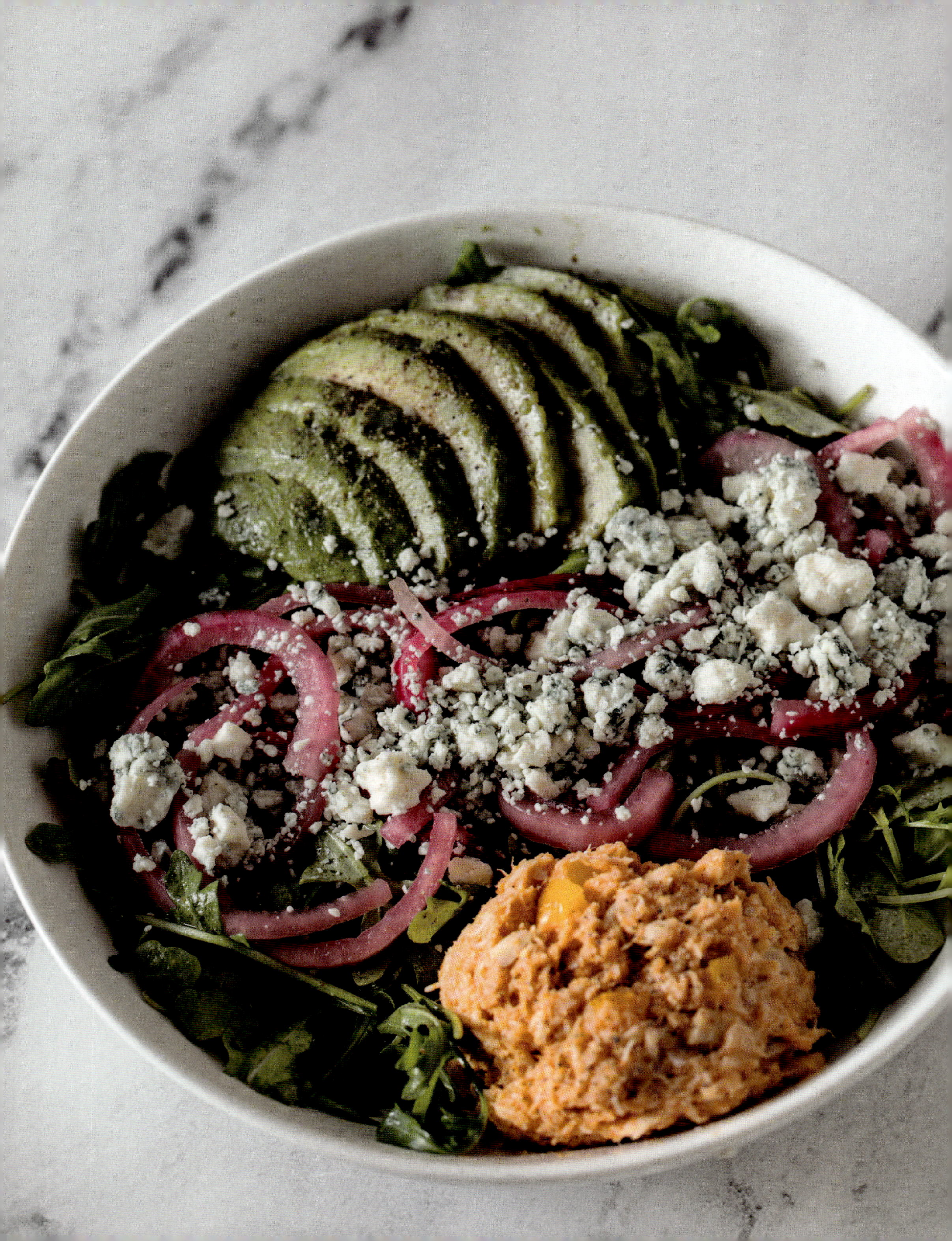

SERVING SIZE 1

HAWTHORNE BOTTLE SHOPPE

GREENS WITH A KICK
ARUGULA SALAD WITH SRIRACHA TUNA

SRIRACHA TUNA
- 8 ounces Albacore tuna, drained
- 2 ½ tbsp Sriracha
- 1 tbsp extra virgin olive oil
- ½ fresh squeezed lemon
- ¼ cup diced yellow pepper
- Salt and freshly ground black pepper

ARUGULA SALAD
- 2 ½ cups arugula
- 2 tsp olive oil
- 2 tsp lemon juice
- Salt and freshly ground black pepper
- 2 tbsp blue cheese crumbles
- 2 tbsp pickled red onions

Hawthorne Bottle Shoppe is a neighborhood, social establishment and market dedicated to the education and enjoyment of craft beer, wine and local deli offerings. All vegetables at the shoppe are sourced from a St. Pete produce vendor several times a week for the freshest product. This simple arugula salad packs a kick with its mayo-less tuna mixture. Test your taste buds with the addition of pickled red onions and blue cheese crumbles.

1. Dice yellow pepper.
2. Drain tuna and place in small mixing bowl.
3. Combine all Sriracha Tuna ingredients into mixing bowl, season with salt and pepper to taste, set aside.
4. Place arugula in serving bowl.
5. Mix olive oil and lemon juice, toss arugula in olive oil and lemon juice.
6. Season with salt and freshly ground black pepper.
7. Top with blue cheese crumbles and pickled red onions.
8. Add tuna mixture to salad.

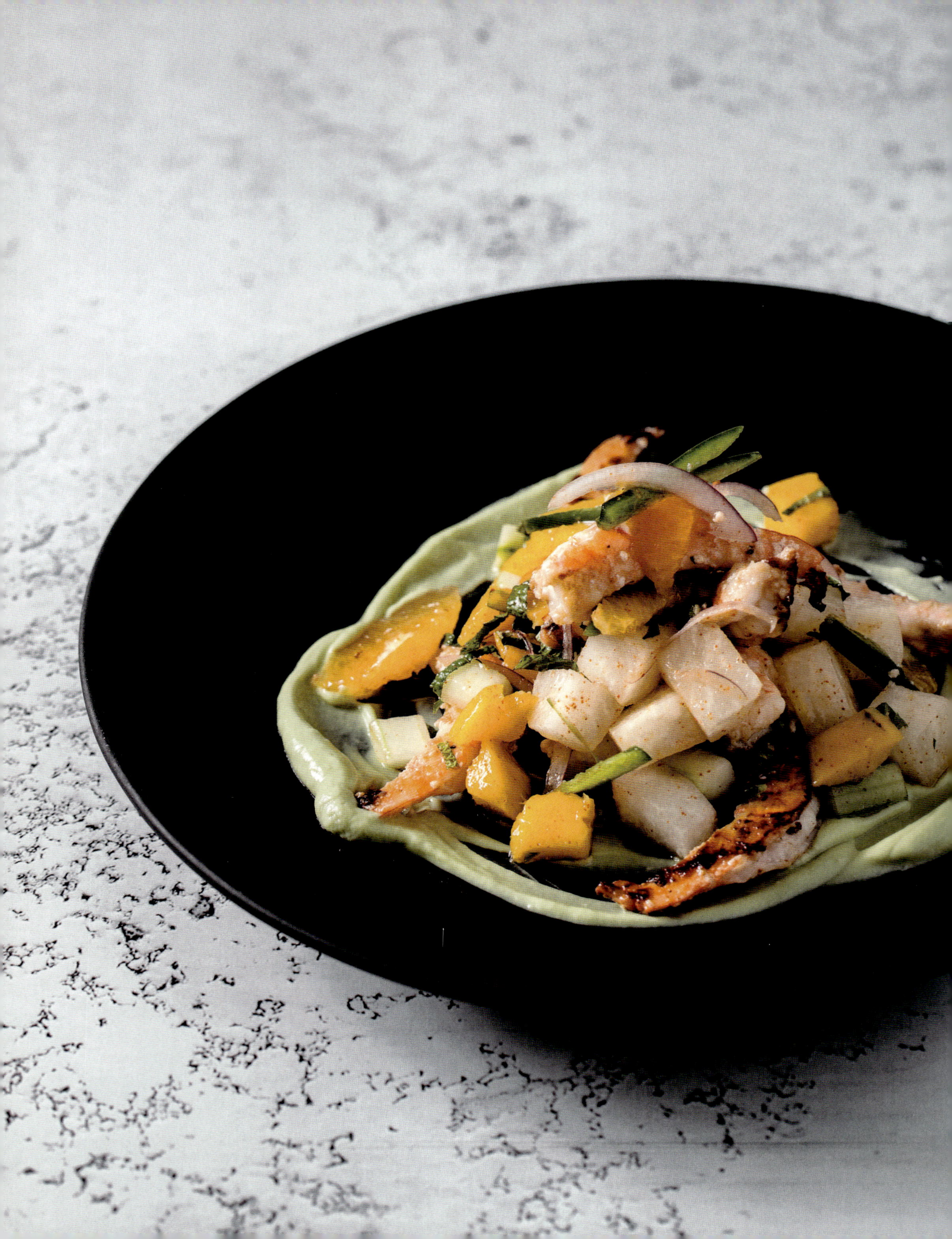

SERVING SIZE 4

RED MESA

MANGO & JICAMA SALAD
WITH LOCALLY-SOURCED SHRIMP

- 2 cups diced mango, about 1 inch
- 2 cups diced jicama root, about 1 inch
- 1 cup diced cucumber, about 1 inch
- ¼ cup of julienne red onion
- 1 jalapeño pepper, remove seeds and thinly julienne
- 2 Florida oranges, use the segments only, and juice the rest of the orange and set aside
- ½ cup chiffonade mint
- 1 lb. medium local shrimp
- Juice of 3 limes
- 3 tsp kosher salt
- 1 tsp coarse black pepper
- 1 tsp cayenne pepper
- 1 avocado

Red Mesa serves regional Mexican as well as many other Latin American specialties. The menu highlights favorites from 20+ years of continuous culinary exploration. This salad recipe can serve as an appetizer or entree depending on portion size. Fresh mango and jicama paired with delicious locally-sourced shrimp, makes this salad of contrasting flavors work together harmoniously.

1. In a mixing bowl, combine mango, cucumber, jicama, red onion, jalapeño, mint, juice of 1 lime, juice from the oranges, cayenne pepper and 1 tsp of kosher salt. Toss well. Set aside.
2. Peel and devein shrimp.
3. Season shrimp with 1 tsp kosher salt and black pepper.
4. Cook shrimp on the grill or in a sautée pan each for about 2 minutes per side, then set aside to briefly cool.
5. Add shrimp to mango mixture and toss again.
6. Using the blender, purée the avocado with 1 tsp kosher salt and the juice of the 2 remaining limes.
7. Place a spoonful of avocado purée on the middle of the plate, forming a circle. Top with the shrimp and mango mixture.

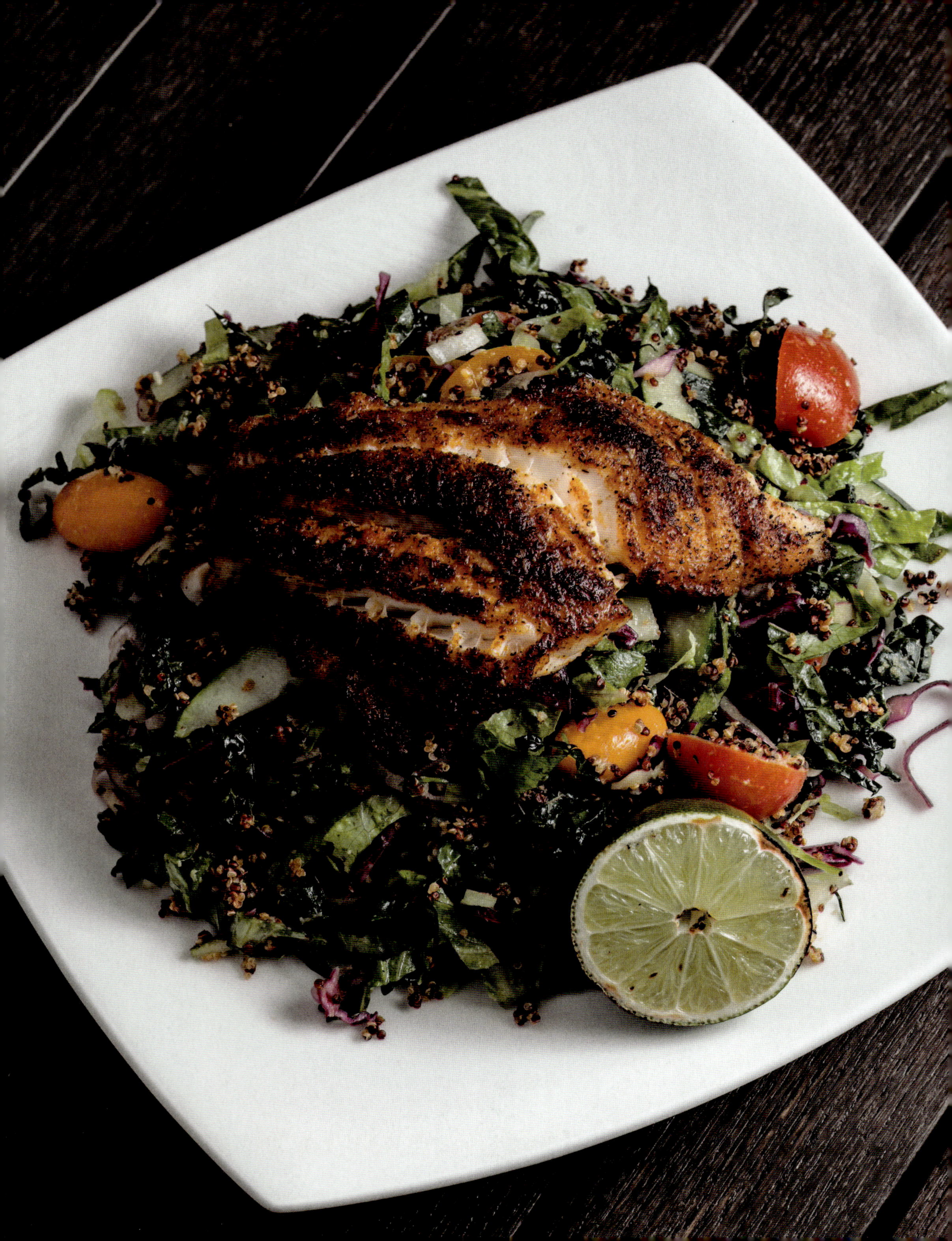

SERVING SIZE 2

TROPHY FISH

BEST DRESSED CATCH

BLACKENED SNAPPER AND CRISPY QUINOA SALAD

DRESSING
1 tbsp fresh garlic, minced
2 tbsp fresh ginger, minced
¼ cup cilantro, chopped
¼ cup scallion, chopped
½ cup fresh pineapple, chopped
1 cup lemongrass, chopped
½ cup unseasoned rice vinegar
2 cups sunflower oil
Salt and pepper to taste

CRISPY QUINOA
1 cup dry tricolor quinoa
1 ¾ cup water
Pinch of salt

FISH
2 8-ounce pieces of fresh American Red Snapper fillet (or any flaky white fish)
2 tbsp low sodium blackened seasoning (or any preferred seasoning)
1 tbsp sunflower oil
1 whole lime

SALAD
3 cups tuscan kale, ribs removed and cut into thin strips
3 cups romaine lettuce, cut into thin strips
½ cup cherry tomatos, halved
½ cup cucumbers, seeded and chopped
1 cup red cabbage, shaved
¼ cup red onion, shaved

Trophy Fish is all about local seafood from local fisherman, with recipes highlighting the fresh catch of the day. Although this recipe seems quite intricate, it all comes down to time management. Have all of your ingredients measured out beforehand for easy access to each step. Be sure to wash all of your produce before cooking. Finally, season to your liking.

1. Add all dressing ingredients except the sunflower oil to a blender.
2. Once a purée forms, slowly drizzle in the sunflower oil to emulsify the dressing.
3. Season to taste, set aside.
4. Bring water to a boil in a small saucepan, then stir in quinoa and salt.
5. Reduce heat to a simmer, put on lid and cook 15 minutes.
6. Set oven broiler to high and place one rack to the upper third part of the oven.
7. When the quinoa is cooked, lay it out on a sheet pan.
8. Broil the quinoa, stirring every minute or two, until golden brown and crispy.
9. While quinoa is cooking, preheat oven to 400 degrees.
10. Bring an oven-safe, nonstick skillet up to medium high heat.
11. Season the snapper on both sides.
12. Add oil to the hot skillet then add snapper.
13. Cook for 1 minute then place skillet in oven. Cook until the fish reads an internal temperature of 145 degrees, around 6 to 8 minutes.
14. Remove the fish from the pan to rest on a plate. Zest and juice the lime onto the cooked snapper.
15. Assemble all salad ingredients into large bowl, dress to your preference, top with blackened snapper.

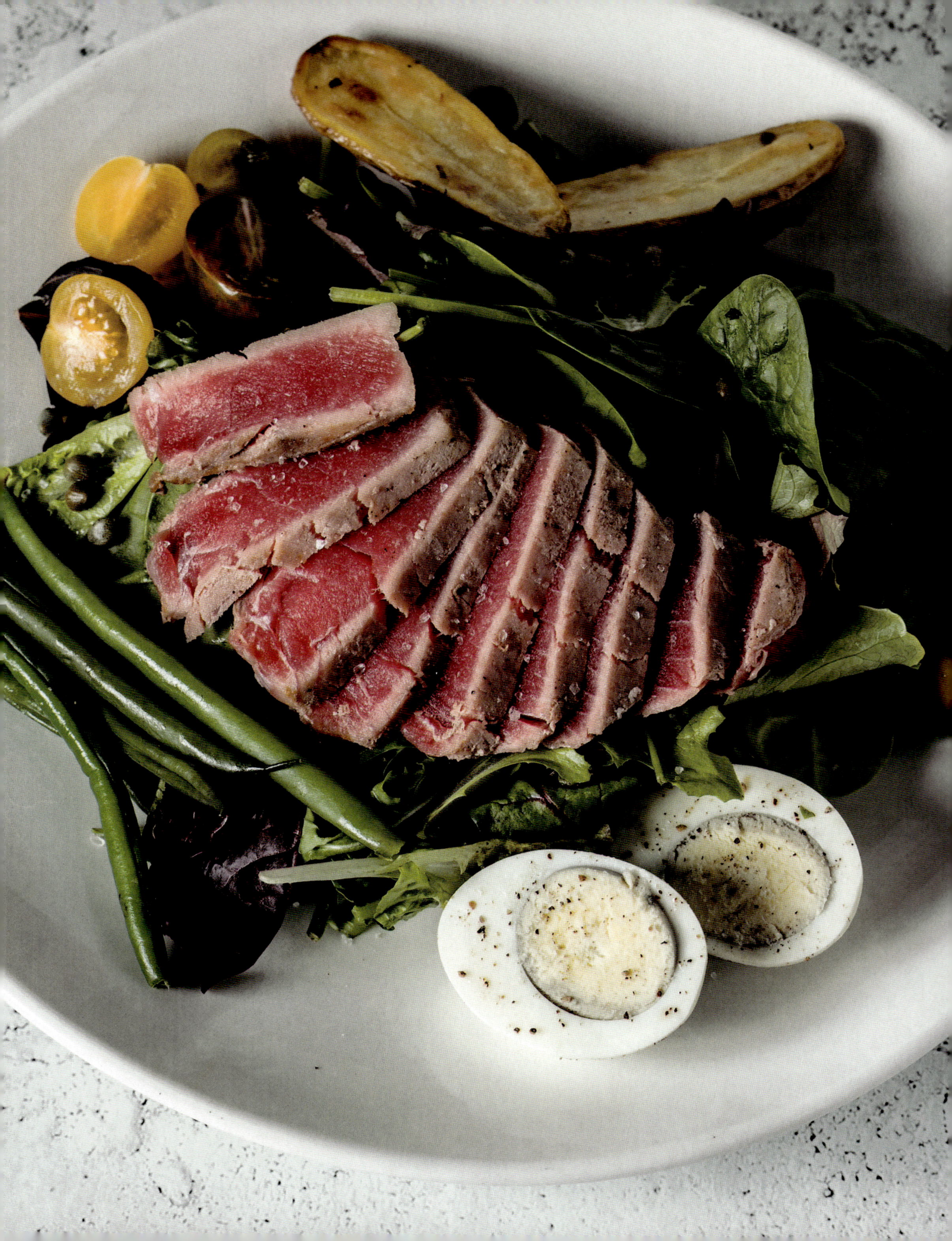

SERVING SIZE 4

THE LEFT BANK BISTRO
NICOISE SALAD
GLUTEN-FREE TUNA SALAD

ROASTED POTATOES
5 red potatoes, quartered
Olive oil
Dry tarragon
Salt and pepper

TUNA PREP
4 ounces tuna
Olive oil
Salt and pepper

DRESSING
1 ounce champagne vinegar
2 ounces red wine vinegar
1 shallot, roasted
1 tsp honey
¾ cup light olive oil

ASSEMBLY INGREDIENTS
1 egg, hard boiled
5 olives, pitted
5 green beans, blanched
4 cherry tomato, halved
1 tsp capers
2 cups mixed greens

The Left Bank Bistro transports diners back to the 1920s on the Seine, creating a place for craft cocktails and French dishes. Using the best ingredients, The Left Bank Bistro proudly serves locally-sourced and sustainable products on its menu.

Roasted Potatoes
1. Quarter potatoes, toss in olive oil, salt, pepper, and dry tarragon.
2. Roast in the oven at 350 degrees for 10 minutes.

Dressing
1. In a blender, add everything except the olive oil.
2. Blend ingredients then drizzle the olive oil slowly.
3. Set aside.

Tuna
1. Lightly season tuna with salt and pepper.
2. Heat olive oil in a pan, hot but not smoking.
3. Place the tuna in the pan. Sear for about 1 minute (until you get some color), flip and repeat but for only 30 seconds.
4. Place on a plate and let cool in the refrigerator.

Assembly
1. Place mixed greens in the center of a plate.
2. Arrange the ingredients in groups around the greens.
3. Slice the tuna thinly and fan out over the greens.
4. Drizzle the dressing over the salad.
5. Season with coarse salt and cracked pepper.

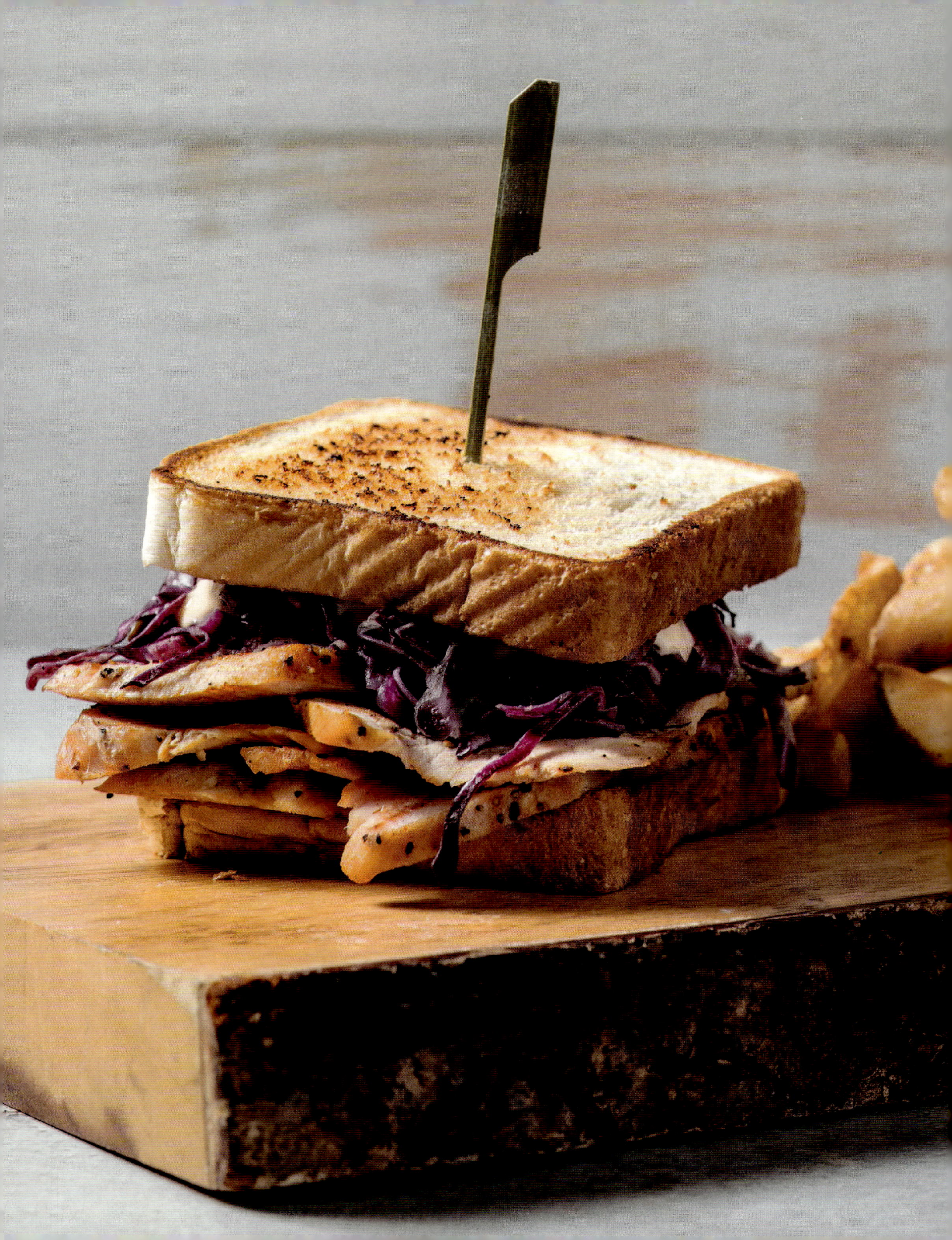

SERVING SIZE 4

DR. BBQ

CALL ME TURKEY
SMOKED TURKEY BREAST WITH PURPLE COLESLAW

Offering "new American barbeque" to the Tampa Bay area, *Dr. BBQ* sizzles with global flavors. The real life Dr. BBQ, Ray Lampe, created these exclusive new recipes by drawing on inspiration from his travels and the local tastes of St. Pete.

- 2 ounces unsalted butter
- 24 ounces smoked turkey breast, sliced to preference
- 8 ounces purple coleslaw (recipe follows)
- 8 ounces smoked tomato aioli (recipe follows)
- 8 slices Texas Toast

PURPLE COLESLAW
- 2 ½ lbs. shredded red cabbage, cut into ⅛ inch pieces
- ½ bunch cilantro, coarsely chopped
- ¼ lb. carrots, shredded
- ¼ lb. maple syrup
- ¼ cup apple cider vinegar
- 1 ¼ tbsp kosher salt
- 1 ¼ tbsp ground black salt
- 1 ¼ cup vegetable oil
- ½ ounce fresh jalapenos, finely diced
- ½ ounce green onions, coarsely chopped
- ¼ tbsp granulated garlic
- ¼ cup toasted pepitas

SMOKED TOMATO AIOLI
- ¾ lb. roma tomato
- ½ ounce vegetable oil
- ¼ gram mayonnaise
- ¼ tbsp garlic cloves
- ¼ ounce kosher salt
- ¼ tbsp ground black pepper

Smoked Tomato Aioli
1. In a medium bowl, toss tomatoes with the vegetable oil, salt, and pepper, then place on a pan and put in your smoker until tomatoes are soft and have a red brown color.
2. Place tomatoes in food processor with garlic and purée until smooth.
3. Add purée to mayonnaise and whisk until blended.
4. Wrap and refrigerate until ready to use.

Purple Coleslaw
1. Combine ingredients and toss thoroughly.
2. Cover and refrigerate until ready to use.

Assembly
1. Using a non-stick pan or griddle, melt the butter and toast one side of each piece of bread.
2. Spread even amounts of tomato aioli on all sides of untoasted bread.
3. Stack sliced smoked turkey on each sandwich followed by 2 ounces of purple slaw on top of each sandwich, then top with top slice of bread.
4. Cut in half.

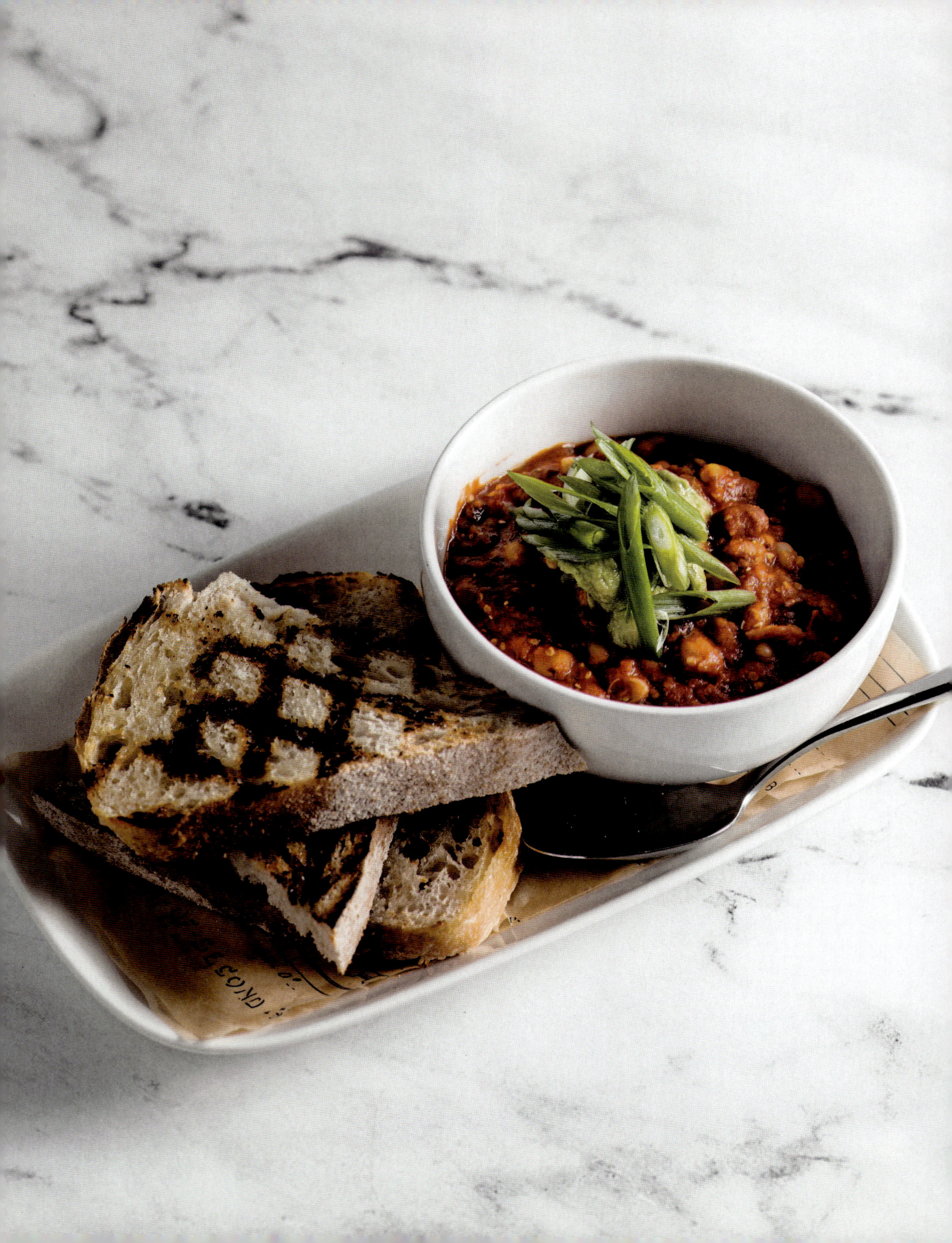

SERVING SIZE 4

THE LIBRARY

VEGETARIAN CHILI
GARNISHED WITH CHOPPED CILANTRO

Half yellow onion, diced
1 red pepper, deseeded and diced
1 fresh corn, cut kernels off cob
1 poblano, deseed and diced
1 tbsp minced garlic
3 tbsp olive oil
3 tbsp tomato paste
¾ tbsp chili powder
1 tbsp smoked paprika
¾ tbsp cumin
Pinch of cayenne
1 can kidney beans
1 can navy beans
1 can garbanzo beans
1 can black beans
1 can roma tomatoes
2 cans crushed tomatoes
2 ounces hemp seeds
3 tbsp Cholula hot sauce
2 tbsp smoked sea salt
½ tbsp salt and pepper
1 cup chopped cilantro

The Library, located on the Johns Hopkins All Children's Hospital campus, offers a menu curated by James Beard semifinalist Chef Rachel Bennett.

1. In a large stockpot, add the onion, red pepper, corn kernels, poblanos, and olive oil. Cook until vegetables are soft.
2. Add tomato paste to vegetables and cook for 2 minutes.
3. Add chili powder, smoked paprika, cumin, and cayenne. Cook for 2 minutes while constantly stirring to allow spices to bloom.
4. Drain and rinse the kidney beans, garbanzos, black beans, and navy beans. Add the beans to the saute mixture.
5. Add tomatoes.
6. Reduce heat to a simmer and allow to cook for 1.5 to 2 hours.
7. After cooking is done, add the hemp seeds, Cholula, smoked sea salt, salt, and pepper.
8. Remove 2 cups of the chili and blend it in a blender, then add back to the original chili.
9. Finish chili with 1 cup of chopped cilantro.

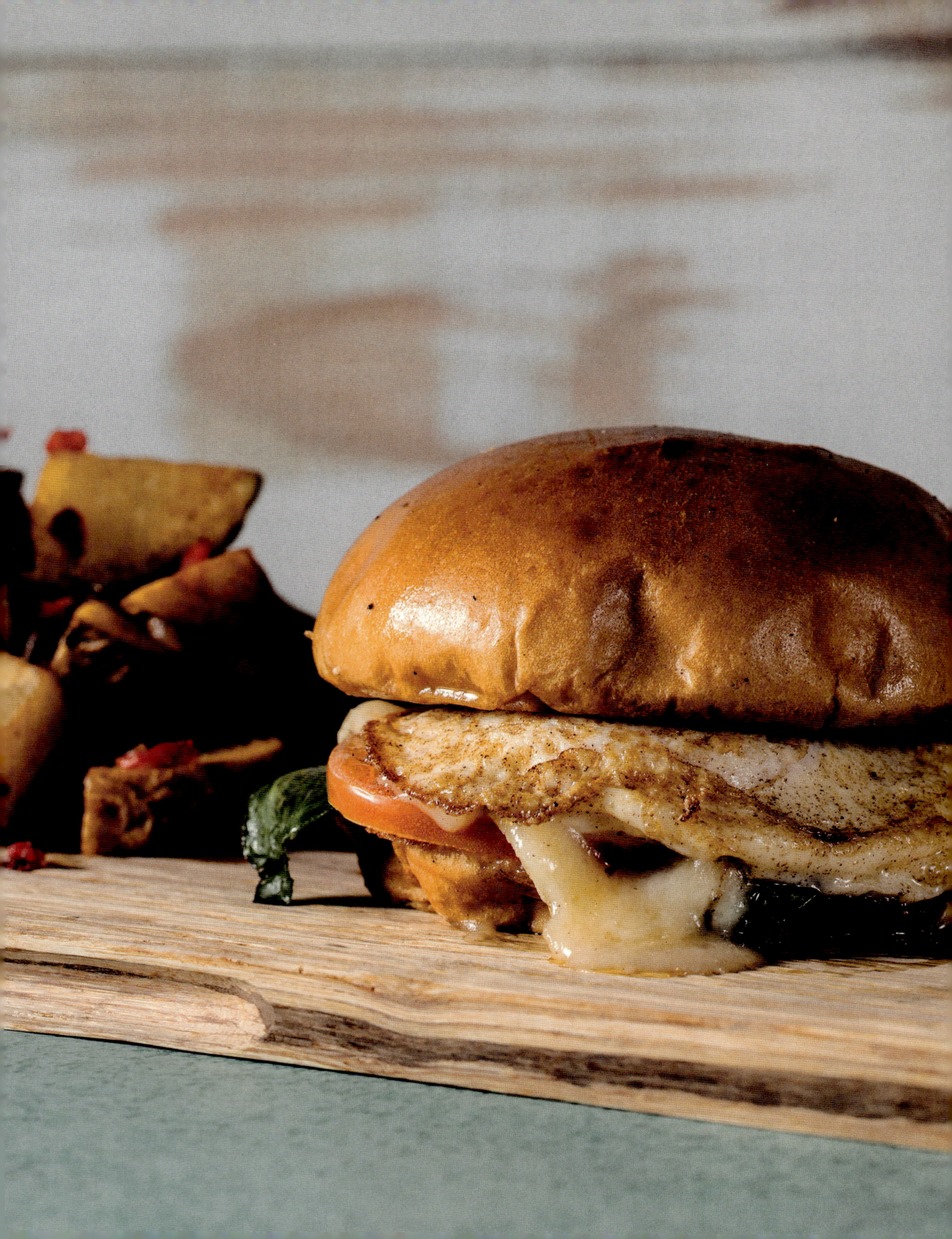

SERVING SIZE 4

DATZ
BRIE BARDOT SANDWICH
LOADED WITH EGGS, SPINACH AND BRIE CHEESE

- 4 4.5-inch challah buns
- 3 ounces fresh baby spinach
- 2 ripe red tomatoes, sliced
- 12 ounces brie cheese, sliced into 3 ounce portions
- 2 ounces unsalted butter
- 4 large eggs

Since the opening of **Datz** in 2009, owners Roger and Suzanne Perry have aimed to reinvent Tampa's food scene. Focusing on comfort food with flair, Datz also concentrates on craft beer and bourbon on its eclectic cocktail menu.

1. In a large non-stick skillet, place half of the butter and melt completely.
2. Crack the eggs, breaking the yolks after the eggs start to set.
2. Using a non-stick pan, or griddle, melt the remaining butter and place the buns cut side down to toast.
3. Flip the eggs, evenly divide and place spinach on top. Evenly top with cheese and place in toaster oven until cheese is melted and egg is cooked to desired doneness.
4. Place egg, cheese, and spinach on top of bottom bun, then top with tomato slices and top bun.
5. Serve immediately.

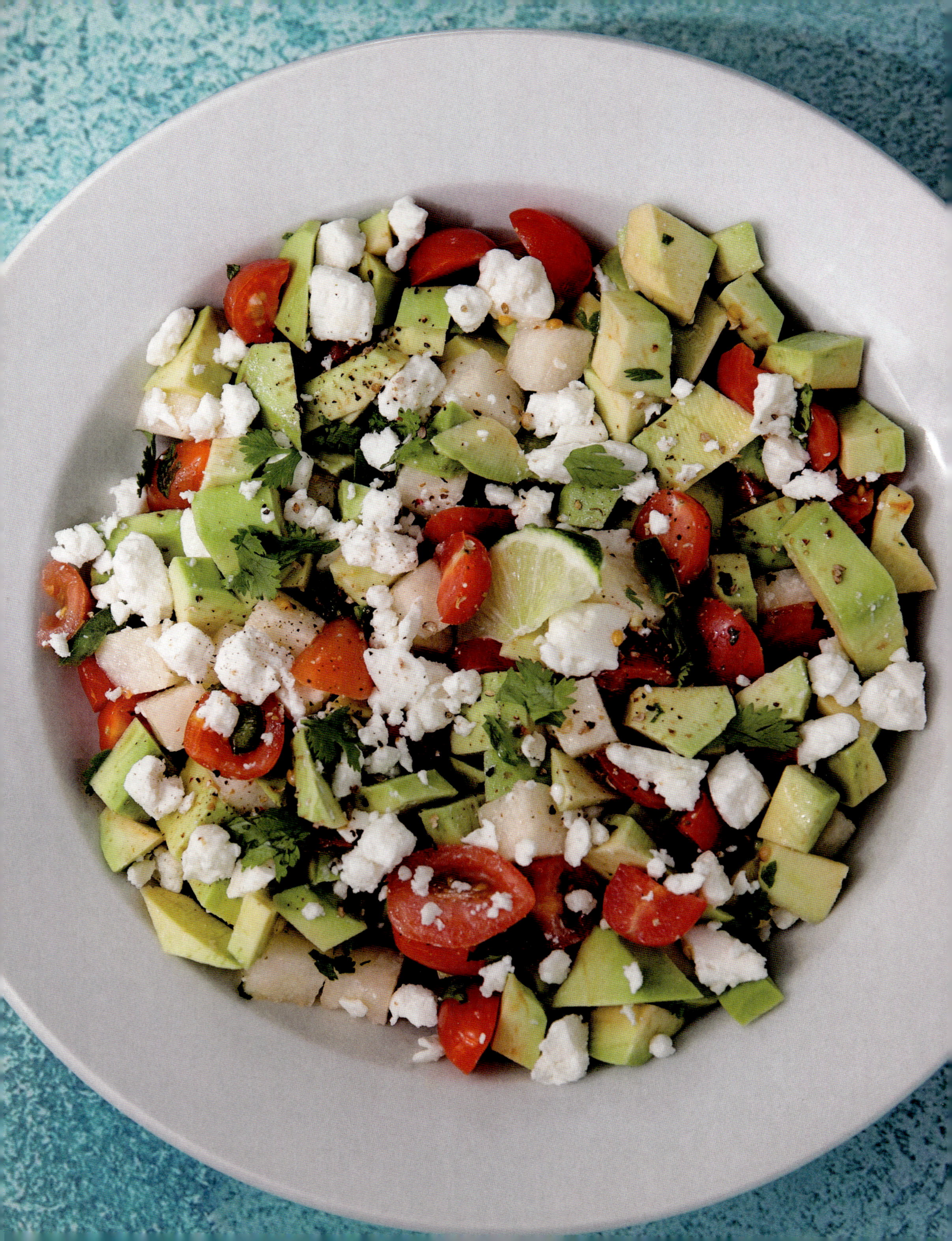

SERVING SIZE 4-6

DR. KANIKA TOMALIN'S JICAMA AVOCADO SALAD

WITH A SPICY JALAPEÑO KICK

1 medium ripe avocado
½ cup jicama, chopped
½ cup cherry tomatoes
¼ cup chopped cilantro
½ cup feta cheese
1 jalapeño, diced (optional)
Juice of half a lime
1 tbsp light olive oil or Italian dressing
Salt and pepper

This a great summer salad that takes avocado to the next level. The crisp crunch of jicama, combined with the freshness of cilantro and spicy kick of fresh jalapeño, makes for an awesome guilt-free meal that you'll enjoy every time you make it.

1. Chop all ingredients into bite-sized chunks.
2. Fold together, mixing in olive oil and lime juice.
3. Season to taste with salt and pepper.
4. Serve immediately.

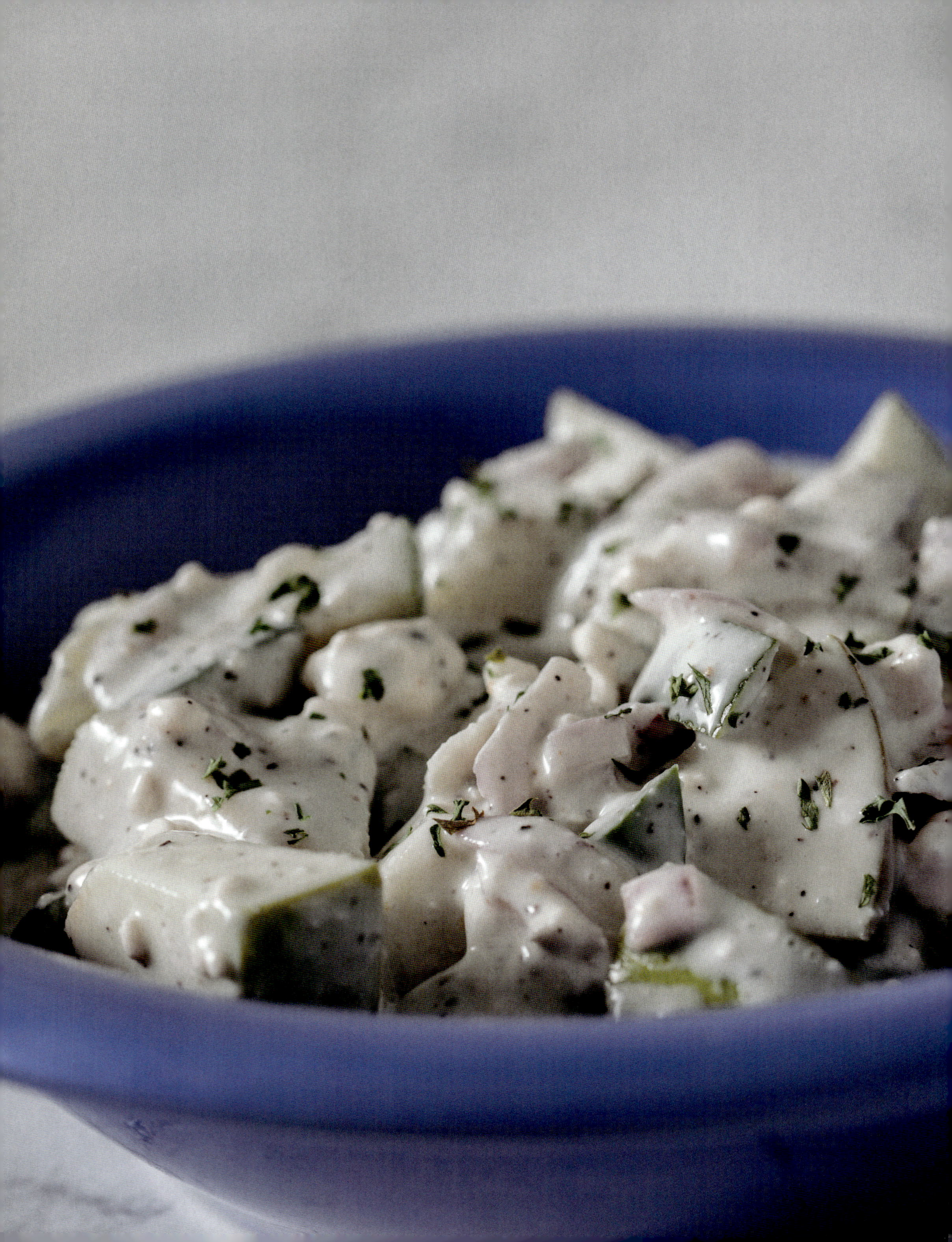

SERVING SIZE 10

PUNKY'S BAR AND GRILL

GREEN APPLE CUCUMBER SALAD
REFRESHING SIDE WITH BLUE CHEESE CRUMBLES

3 green apples, thinly sliced
3 cucumbers, thinly sliced
½ red onion, thinly sliced
1 cup blue cheese crumbles
2 to 3 cups blue cheese dressing

Punky's Bar and Grill is home to live music, DJs, weekend drag shows and a variety of menu items including unique appetizers, flatbreads and burgers. Located in the Grand Central District, Punky's is also the perfect spot to enjoy weekend brunch with friends.

1. Combine all ingredients in medium sized bowl, mix well.
2. Chill before serving.

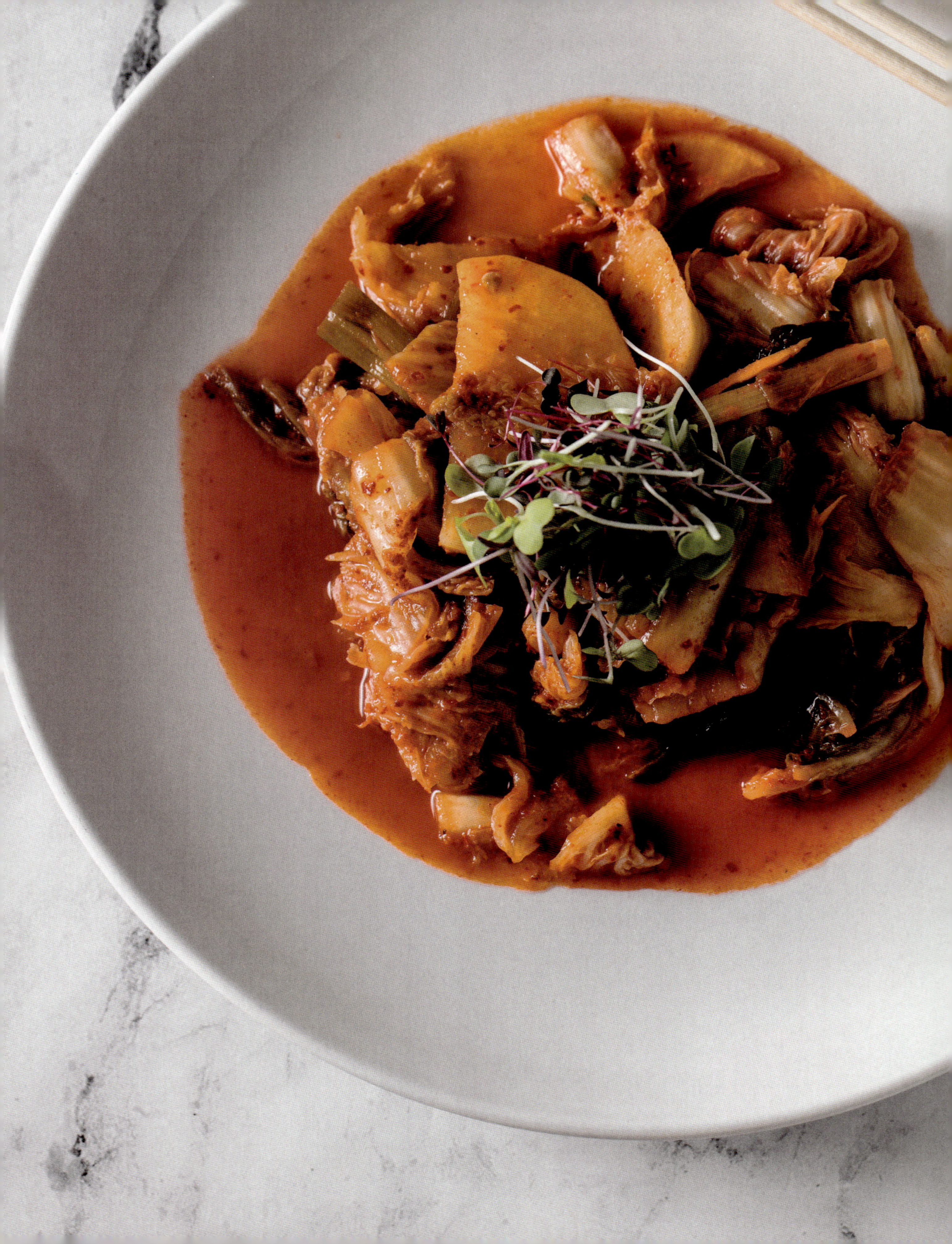

SERVING SIZE 2-4

PACIFIC COUNTER

PC KIMCHI
FERMENTED VEGETABLES

- 3 medium size napa cabbages
- 1 ¼ cups coarse rock salt
- 1 ½ cups water
- 1 Korean radish mu (about 1 ½ pounds)
- 1 tbsp coarse sea salt
- 7 bunches scallions, roughly chopped

SEASONING
- 2 cups of water
- 2 cups gochugaru Korean red chili pepper flakes
- ½ cup Saeu-jeot shrimp, finely minced
- ½ cup Myeolchi-jeot fish (or anchovy) sauce
- ½ cup minced garlic
- ¼ cup ginger finely grated ginger
- 2 tbsp sugar

Pacific Counter is a fresh fusion of chef-inspired cuisines and cultures, serving up a mainland mix of coastal classics in the form of sushi bowls and burritos. PC Kimchi brings together spicy, sour and umami flavors, and is known for it vast nutritional benefits.

1. Cut the cabbage heads into quarters and remove the core from each quarter. Cut each quarter crosswise into bite sizes (about 1 ½ inches). Place the cabbage pieces in a large bowl.
2. In a smaller bowl, dissolve 1 ¼ cups of salt in 6 cups of water. Pour over the cabbage. Toss well to wet the cabbage pieces evenly with the salt water. Let stand until the white parts are bendable, about 2 hours, turning the cabbage pieces over occasionally.
3. Cut the diakon radish into bite size pieces (about 1 ½ inch square, about ¼-inch thick). Sprinkle with a tablespoon of salt. Toss well. Let it sit for about 30 minutes. Drain. Do not rinse.
4. Mix the chili pepper flakes with the remaining seasoning ingredients along with ¼ cup of water.
5. Rinse the salted cabbage three times and drain to remove excess water.
6. In a large bowl, add the radish, scallions, and seasoning to the salted cabbage. Using a kitchen glove, mix everything well by hand until the cabbage pieces are well coated with the seasoning mix.
7. Place the kimchi in an airtight container or a jar.
8. To get the remaining seasoning from mixing bowl, fill with ½ cup of water, swirling it around in the bowl before pouring it over the kimchi.
9. Leave the kimchi out at room temperature for a day, depending on how quickly you want your kimchi to ferment.
10. Refrigerate for two days.

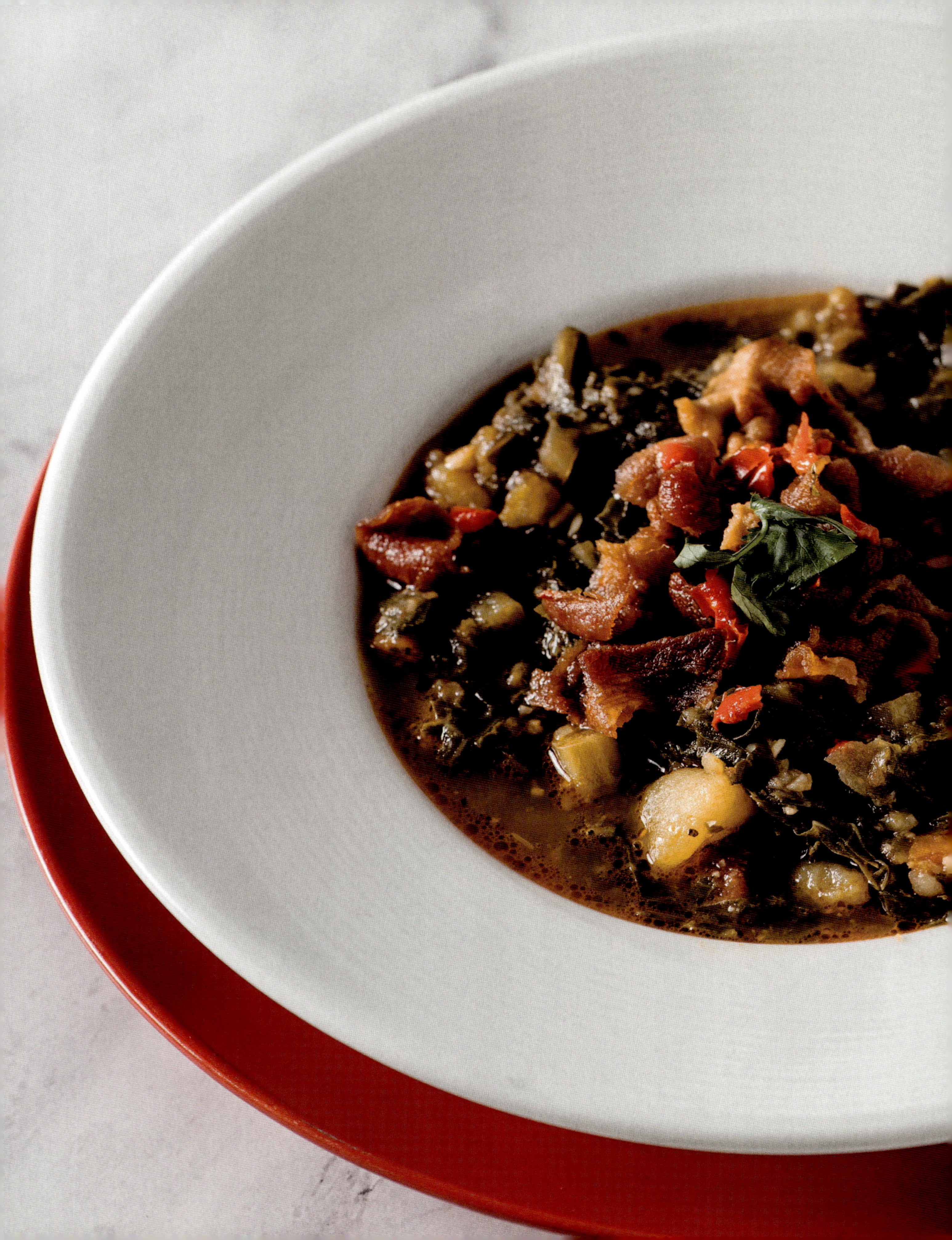

SERVING SIZE 8

CALLALOO

SOUTHERN BRAISED CALLALOO STEW
WITH CRISPY BACON AND VEGGIES

1 pound diced carrots
1 pound diced white onion
1 pound diced celery
1 pound diced potato
½ pound diced bacon
3 ounces diced chopped garlic
3 ounces canola oil
½ gallon braised callaloo greens
1 qt. water
1 tbsp Sazon
1 tsp paprika
3 ounces lemon juice
Salt and pepper to taste

Located at the Historic Manhattan Casino, **Callaloo** blends the best of two worlds by serving Southern comfort foods such as fried chicken and mac 'n cheese while exploring flavors of the islands with mojo style pork and chicken and sweet plantains. Locally distilled spirits and brewed beers are great companions for any meal or to enjoy listening to live music in the lounge.

1. Cook bacon until crispy.
2. Add oil and chopped garlic to bacon and cook until garlic begins to turn brown.
3. Add carrot, onion, and celery and sweat until half-cooked.
4. Add the water to deglaze the bottom of the pan, add callaloo and seasonings.
5. Bring soup to simmer and add diced potato. Simmer stew until potatoes are fully cooked.
6. Finish with lemon juice and add salt and peper to taste.
7. Serve hot in bowl.

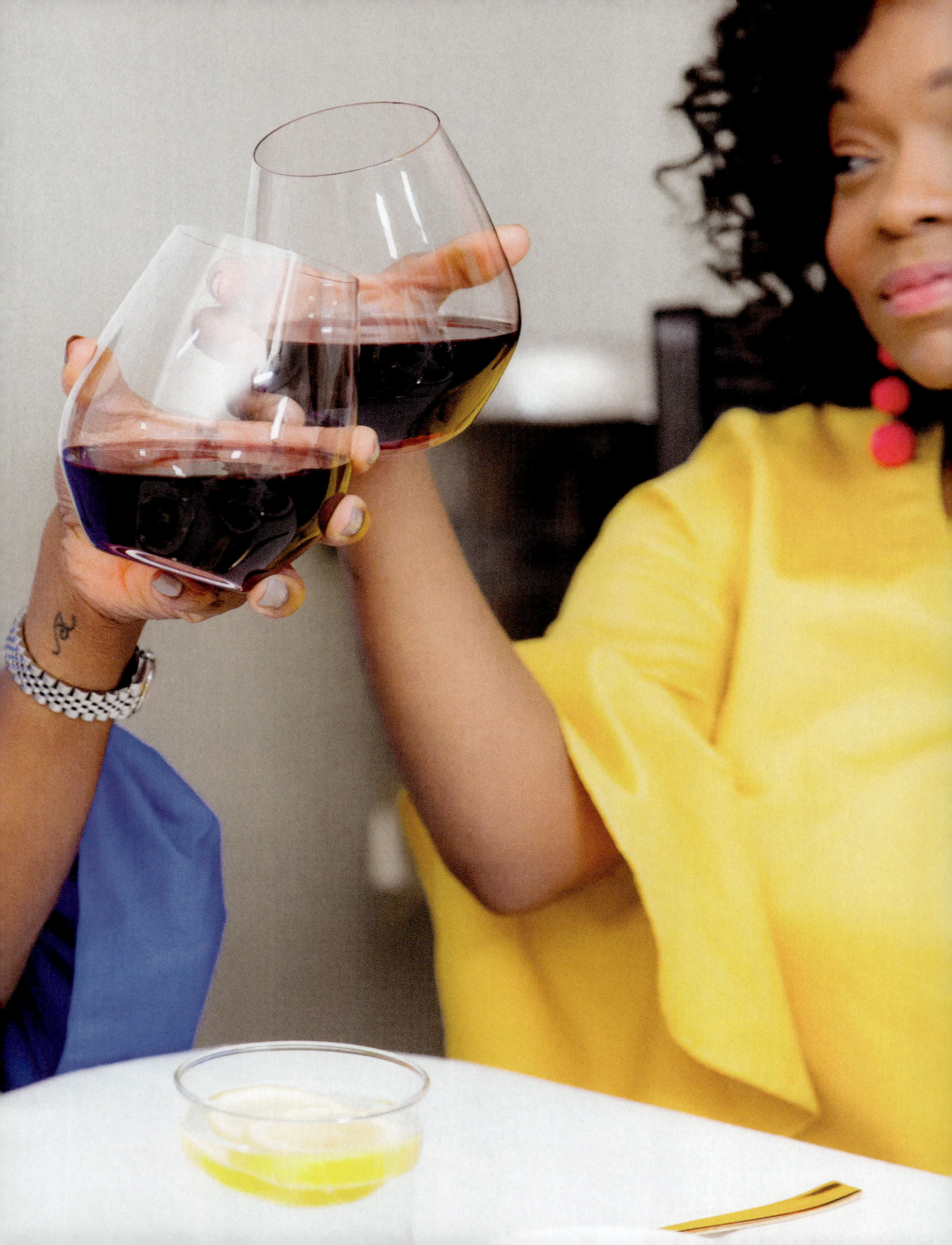

> *As you navigate this cookbook, feel the passion of chefs who are on the cutting edge of St. Pete's culinary scene, and let them guide you through each recipe.*

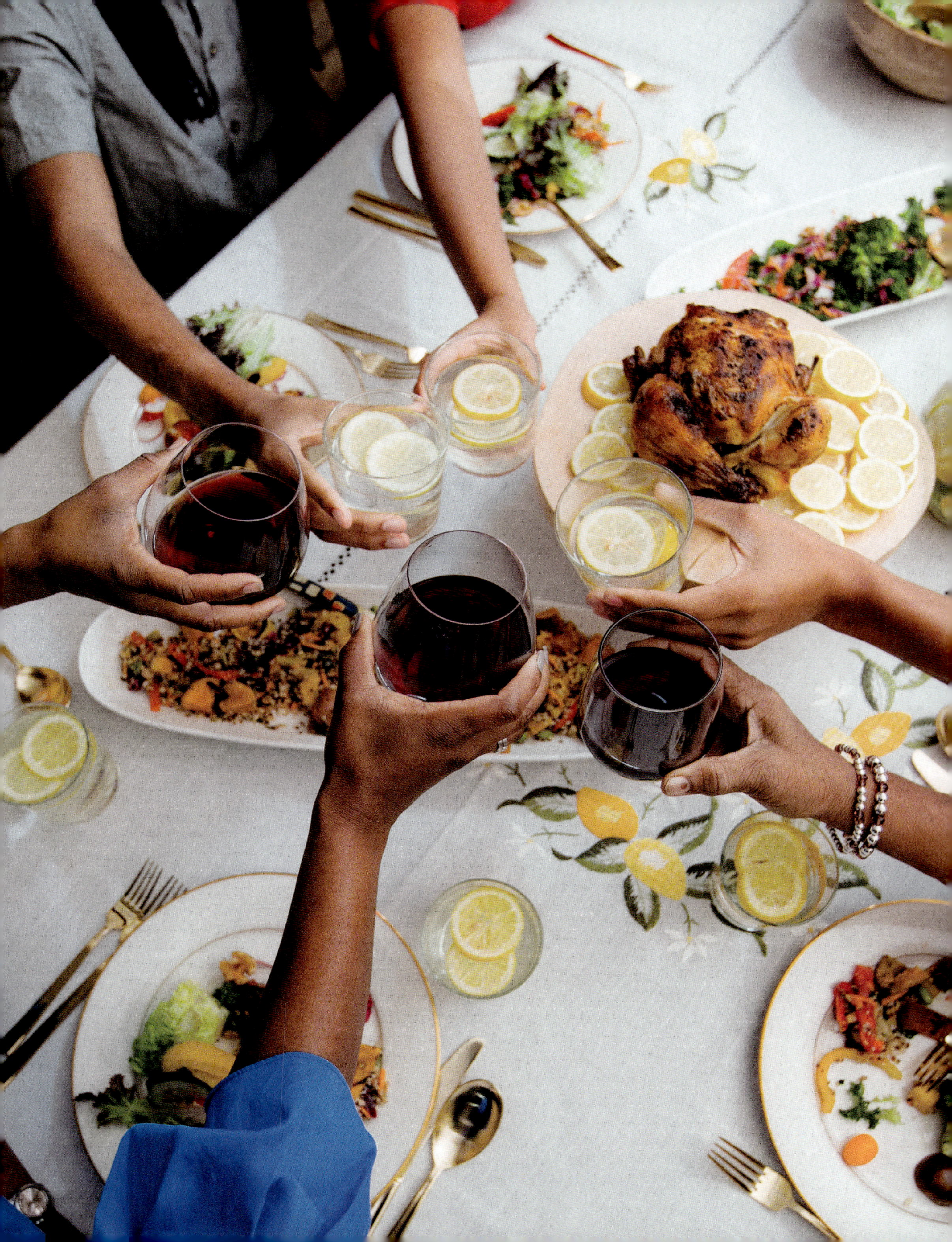

– CHAPTER 3 –
ENTREES

Quite often considered one of the more daunting tasks when it comes to a dinner party, or even a weeknight meal, we can get swept up in the intricacies commonly associated with entree recipes. The beauty of this cookbook is being able to recreate dishes from your favorite local restaurants, or even recipes crafted by St. Pete's top chefs. These step-by-step recipes allow you to relax and enjoy each dish you create.

Throughout my life, I've come to realize that some of my most memorable meals have been simple creations made with love. When my husband and I were first dating, he invited me over for dinner. Initially skeptical of his cooking skills, I indulged him, showing up with an open mind. I sat at his kitchen counter, watching him make zucchini-crusted pizza for us, putting care into every detail from the dough to the sauce to the toppings. Something as simple as a homemade pizza became one of my favorite meals because he'd creatively crafted it with so much love.

If you begin to worry about a specific method, or are still in the process of building confidence in the kitchen, remember it's about the journey. Find joy in creating flavorful meals for the ones you love.

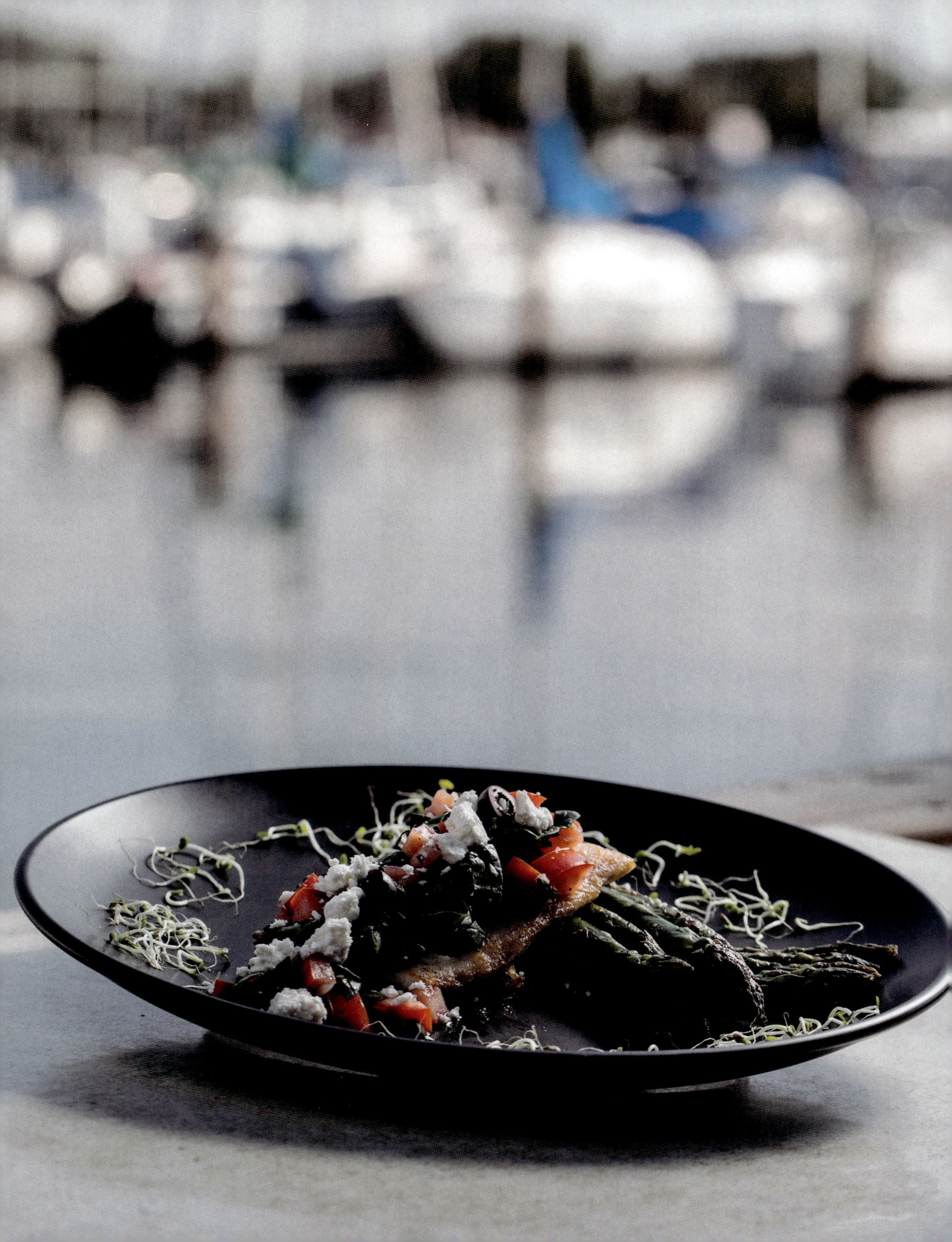

79	DAPPER SNAPPER
81	MAPO TOFU
83	VEGAN ASPARAGUS RISOTTO
85	TASTE OF SOUTHERN ITALY
87	FRESCO FISH
88	TROPICAL TAILS
91	VEGGIE LASAGNA
93	PASTA ARRABBIATA
95	DR. KANIKA TOMALIN'S CLASSIC CAPRESE WITH CHICKEN
97	CAULIFLOWER STEAK
99	ROPA VIEJA
100	BUDDHA BOWL

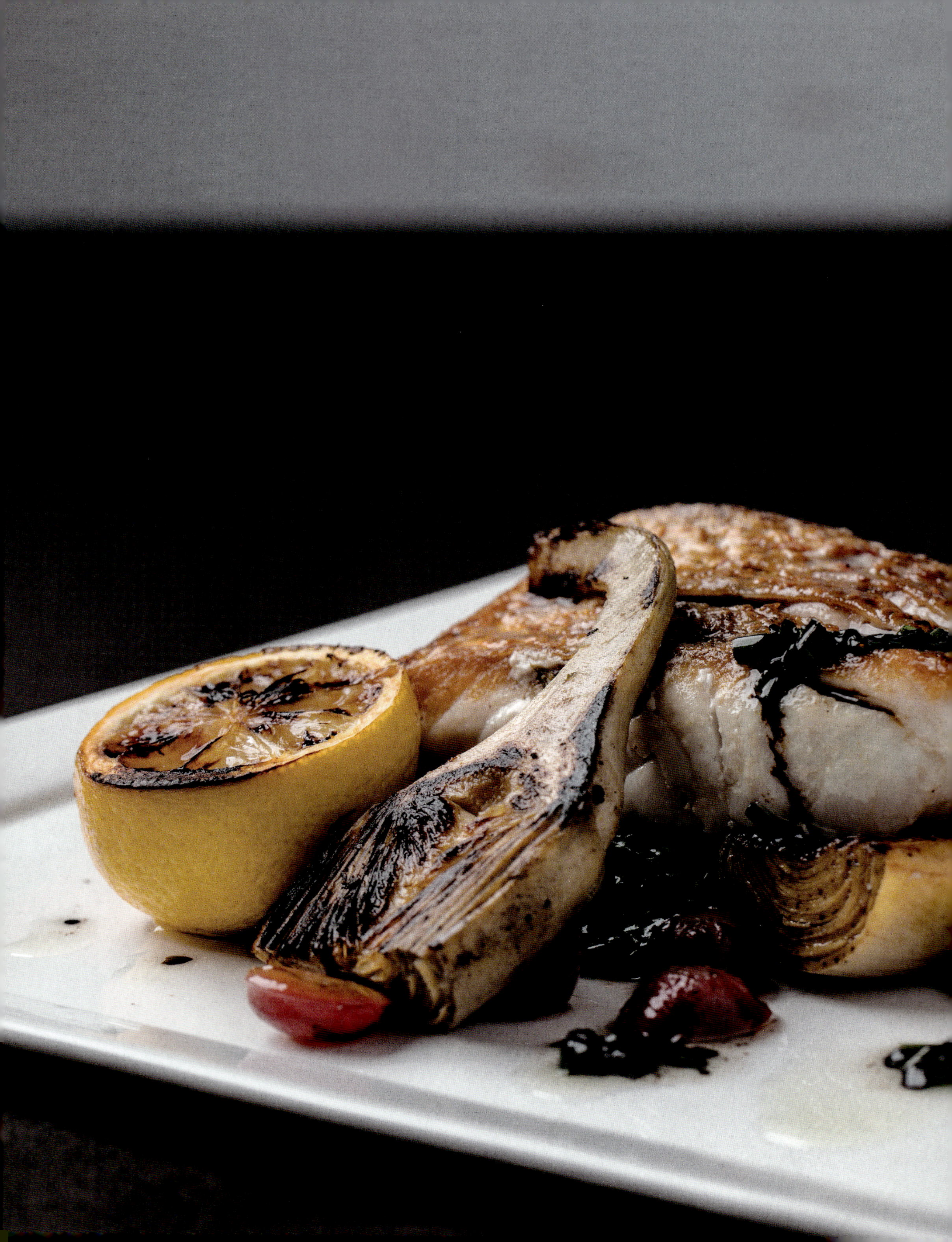

SERVING SIZE 4

SEA SALT

DAPPER SNAPPER
RED SNAPPER WITH TUSCAN KALE, ARTICHOKES, GRAPES AND TRUFFLE VINAIGRETTE

1 lb. kale, roughly chopped
20 red grapes, halved
16 pieces quartered artichoke hearts
½ ounce truffle oil
½ ounce balsamic reduction
Juice of 1 lemon
4 sprigs thyme
1 ounce canola oil
5 ounces fillets of red snapper
1 tbsp of butter
¼ cup of chopped chives
Salt and freshly ground pepper to taste

Sea Salt offers a Venetian touch on Florida's freshest seafood and produce, utilizing organic and local produce, sustainable ingredients from local farmers and day boat fishermen, and poultry and meat raised naturally without hormones, antibiotics or animal-by-products whenever possible. Red snapper is one of Florida's most popular fish. With the addition of healthy produce and a light, low-fat sauce packed full of flavor, who says eating healthy can't be delicious?

1. In a bowl, mix the balsamic reduction with the truffle oil and chives. Set aside.
2. Heat a large sauté pan over medium heat.
3. Add canola oil, kale, grapes, and artichokes, cook for 5 minutes until the kale has wilted. Season with salt and pepper, and set aside.
4. Preheat oven to 400 degrees.
5. Heat a large ovenproof sauté pan over high heat. Add canola oil to the pan, then season the fish fillets on the skin side with salt and pepper.
6. Gently lay the fillets in the hot sauté pan skin side down and cook for 1 minute.
7. Transfer the pan with the fillets to the oven for 4 to 6 minutes. Fish should be opaque in the center when done.
8. To plate, spoon a portion of the kale mixture on each plate, place the fish on top then spoon some of the vinaigrette over the fish and around the plate.
9. Garnish with chopped chives and serve.

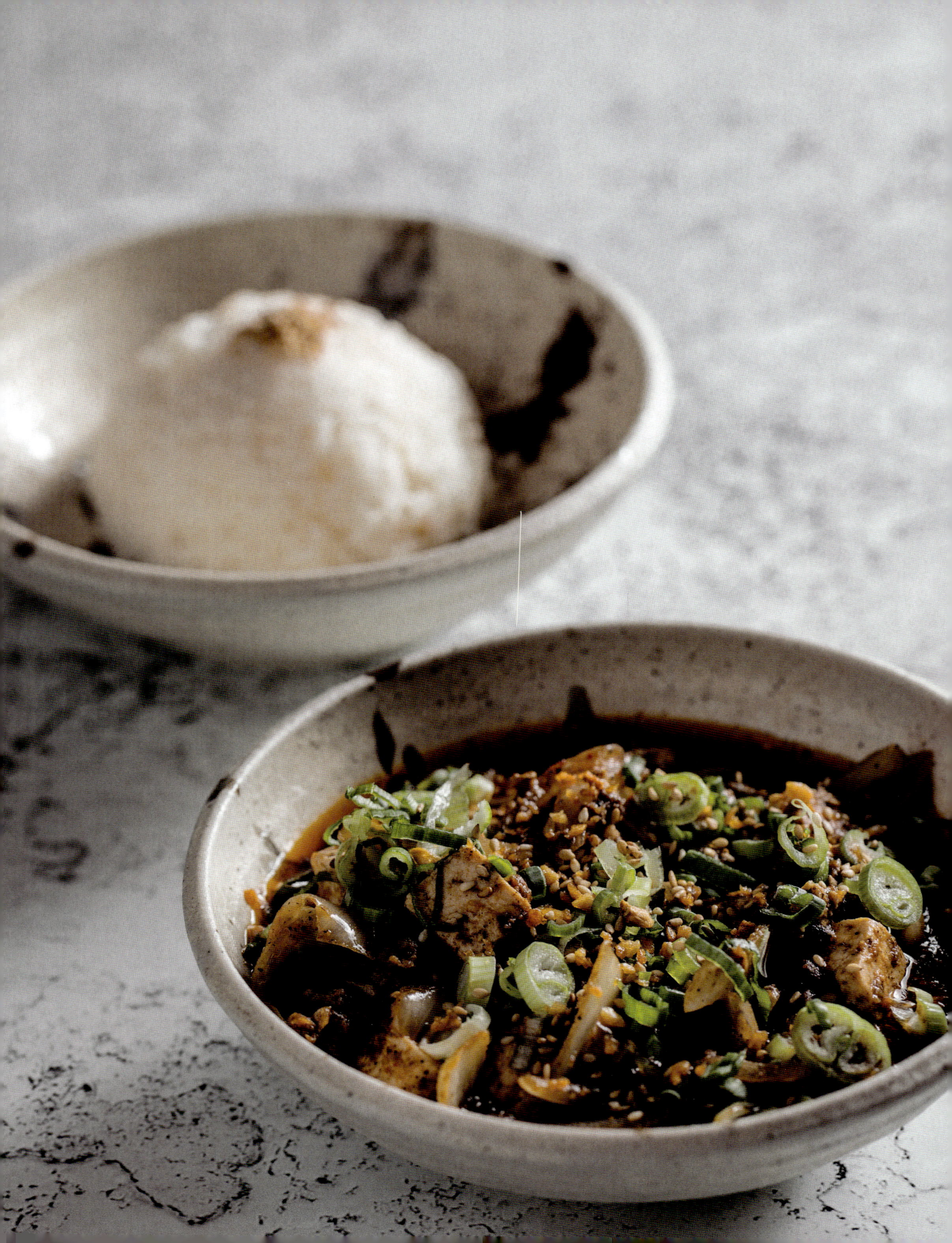

SERVING SIZE 2-4

ICHICORO ANE

MAPO TOFU
VEGATARIAN DISH WITH A LITTLE BIT OF SPICE

1 ounce sesame oil
6 ounces Impossible Burger, sautéed and browned
6 ounces firm tofu, diced into ½ inch pieces
½ white onion sliced, sautéed and browned
1 ounce garlic, puréed
1 ounce ginger, puréed
4 ounces mapo paste (recipe follows)
1 ounce bean sprouts
12 ounces vegetable broth or mushroom broth
4 ounces butter, whole, unsalted
Jasmine rice, cooked
Fried garlic, for garnish
Scallions, sliced thin, for garnish
Toasted white sesame seeds, for garnish

MAPO PASTE
400 grams chili garlic paste
200 grams ginger, puréed
50 grams garlic, puréed
600 grams jalapeños, charred and stemmed
800 grams spicy chili oil
200 grams fermented black beans
50 grams habanero chili
40 grams Szechuan peppercorns
20 grams Sancho peppercorns
40 grams yuzu juice
40 grams salt, Kosher
30 grams sugar, white

Ichicoro Ane is a buzzy, stylish basement-level haunt offering izakaya-style small plates, ramen and creative cocktails. This dish is comprised of mainly tofu, the Impossible Burger and a Szechuan-style paste that gives the dish its classic flavor. This can be a vegan dish if butter is omitted. These ingredients are available from an online grocery or at local oriental markets.

Mapo Paste
1. Combine all ingredients in blender and purée until extremely smooth.
2. Reserve in refrigerator for up to a month.

Mapo Tofu
1. In a saucepan, large 24-fluid ounce capacity, heat on high heat.
2. Add sesame oil and sauté the ginger and garlic until fragrant.
3. Add the onions and the mapo paste and cook until fragrant.
4. Add the previously sautéed Impossible Burger and mushroom broth.
5. Bring to a boil then add the tofu and butter, if desired.
6. Cook for 3 to 5 minutes until mixture thickens slightly.
7. Spoon mixture into bowls divided into 2 to 4 portions.
8. Garnish with scallions and fried garlic.
9. Serve with cooked jasmine rice and toasted sesame seeds.

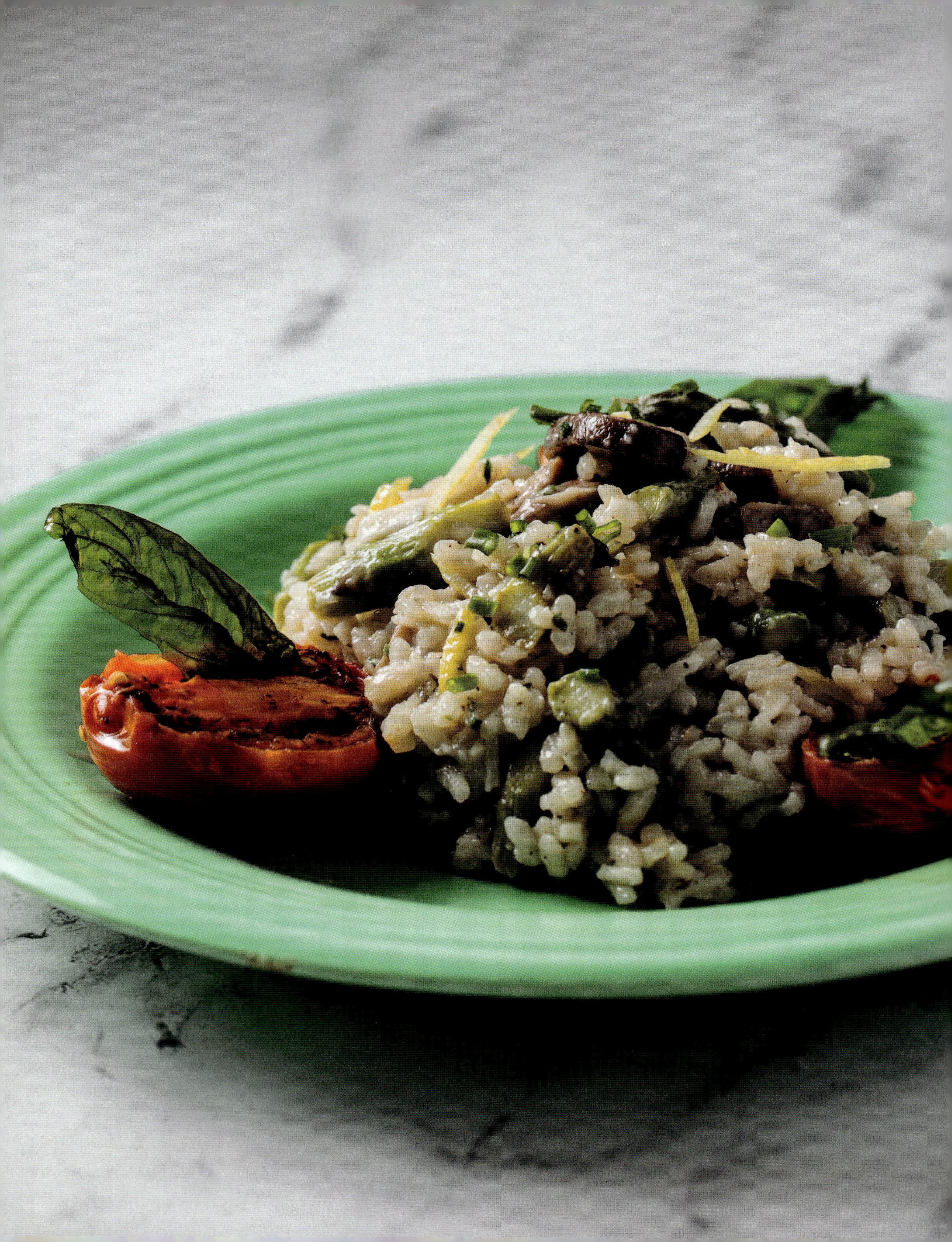

SERVING SIZE 6-8

ROLLIN' OATS

VEGAN ASPARAGUS RISOTTO

CREAMY PLANT-BASED RISOTTO WITH ASPARAGUS

- 3 tbsp Earth Balance buttery spread (or any preferable butter substitute)
- ¼ cup sliced shallots
- 1 ½ cup arborio rice
- 1 cup sliced button mushrooms (substitute shiitake, oyster, crimini, or chanterelle if desired)
- ¼ cup chopped roasted garlic
- ½ cup dry white wine
- 6 cups hot vegetable stock
- ⅓ cups vegan "parmesan cheese" substitute
- 1 tbsp finely grated lemon zest
- 2 cups young asparagus, tips reserved and stalks sliced diagonally about ¼ inch long
- ⅓ cup chopped fresh chives
- Salt and freshly ground black pepper
- Fresh lemon juice, to taste
- Vegan "parmesan cheese" and deep-fried basil sprigs, if desired, to garnish

Rollin' Oats is a locally-owned, natural food market and café serving the Tampa Bay community since 1994. Risotto is a great form of comfort food. The key is to make sure that when the risotto is ready, you serve it immediately. This recipe is a light, healthy, vegan version without the heavy cream that is usually associated with risotto.

1. Melt butter substitute spread in a deep, heavy bottomed saucepan.
2. Add shallots and cook over moderate heat until soft, not brown.
3. Add rice and mushrooms and cook, stirring often until rice is translucent, about 3 minutes.
4. Add garlic, wine and enough stock to cover rice mixture and cook stirring constantly until liquid is nearly absorbed.
5. Continue adding hot stock, stirring constantly and letting the rice absorb the stock before adding more. Begin testing rice after about 12 minutes. The rice needs to be creamy while the center of each grain still has some texture. This will take 16 to 18 minutes total; stir in the asparagus ¾ of the way through.
6. Stir in the zest, chives, and vegan "parmesan cheese" and season to your taste with salt, pepper, and lemon juice.
7. Serve in warm bowls garnished with vegan "parmesan cheese" and fried basil.

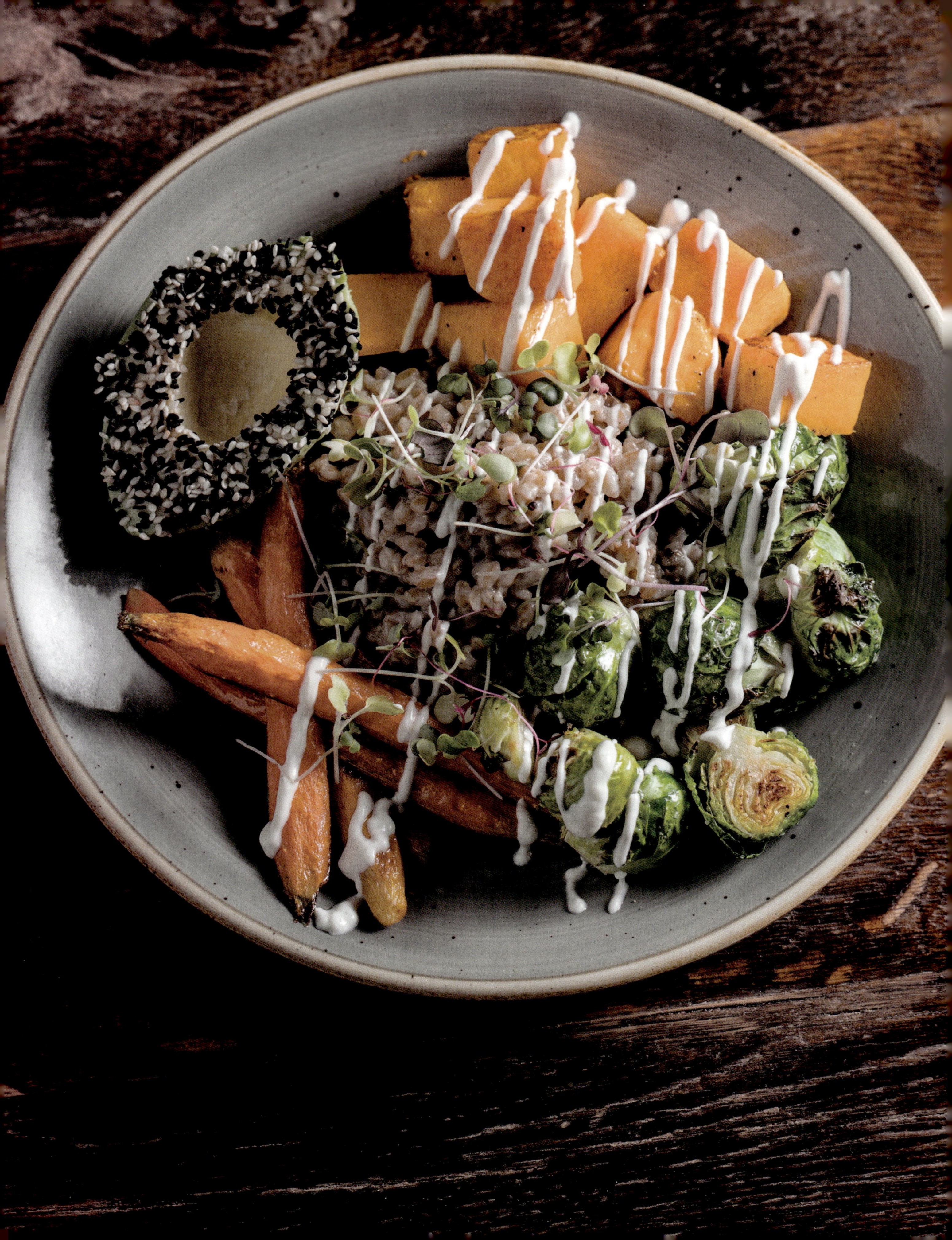

SERVING SIZE 4

FARRO
- 2 tbsp extra virgin olive oil
- 1 tbsp garlic, finely minced
- 2 tbsp shallots, finely minced
- 3 cups farro
- 1 tsp rosemary, finely minced
- 1 tsp thyme, leaves only
- 2 tsps salt
- Fresh cracked black pepper
- ½ cup white wine
- 4 cups water
- 2 tbsp unsalted butter
- ½ lemon, juiced
- 1 tbsp parsley, finely chopped

ROASTED CARROTS
- 1 lb. organic carrots, peeled and cut in half lengthwise
- 2 tbsp olive oil
- 1 pinch of salt
- Fresh cracked black pepper
- 1 tbsp sage, rough chopped
- 2 tbsp honey

LIME YOGURT
- ½ cup plain, greek yogurt
- ½ lime, juiced and zested
- Pinch of salt

SESAME AVOCADO
- 2 avocados, split in half, seeded and skin removed
- 2 tbsp olive oil
- ¼ cup toasted black and white sesame seeds

GARNISH
- 6 ounces micro greens of favorite herbs

NOBLE CRUST

TASTE OF SOUTHERN ITALY

FARRO RISOTTO WITH ROASTED CARROTS, SESAME AND AVOCADO AND LIME YOGURT

Noble Crust is known for seasonal dishes with culinary inspiration from Italian and Southern American cuisine. Farro, an ancient Italian whole grain, cooked in the style of creamy risotto. Served with local carrots roasted in olive oil, honey and sage, the farro is garnished with sesame seed-crusted avocado for texture and color.

Farro
1. Heat a medium pot over low heat and add olive oil, rosemary, thyme, garlic, and shallots. Stir with a spatula and cook for three minutes until garlic softens.
2. Add farro to pot and stir with spatula. Cook for one minute.
3. Increase heat to medium and add white wine. Stir and cook until all wine has evaporated.
4. Add half of the water to the pot and season with salt and pepper. Stir and cook for 15 minutes stirring constantly.
5. Add remaining water and cook for another 20 minutes stirring constantly.
6. Once all water has been absorbed and farro is cooked through but still retains a bite, turn off the heat and stir in butter, lemon juice, and parsley.
7. Spoon farro risotto into four separate bowls.

Roasted Carrots
1. While the farro is cooking, place halved and peeled carrots on a sheet tray.
2. Drizzle olive oil over carrots, sprinkle with chopped sage, and season with salt and pepper. Garnish with microgreens, drizzle with lime yogurt, and serve with sesame avocado.

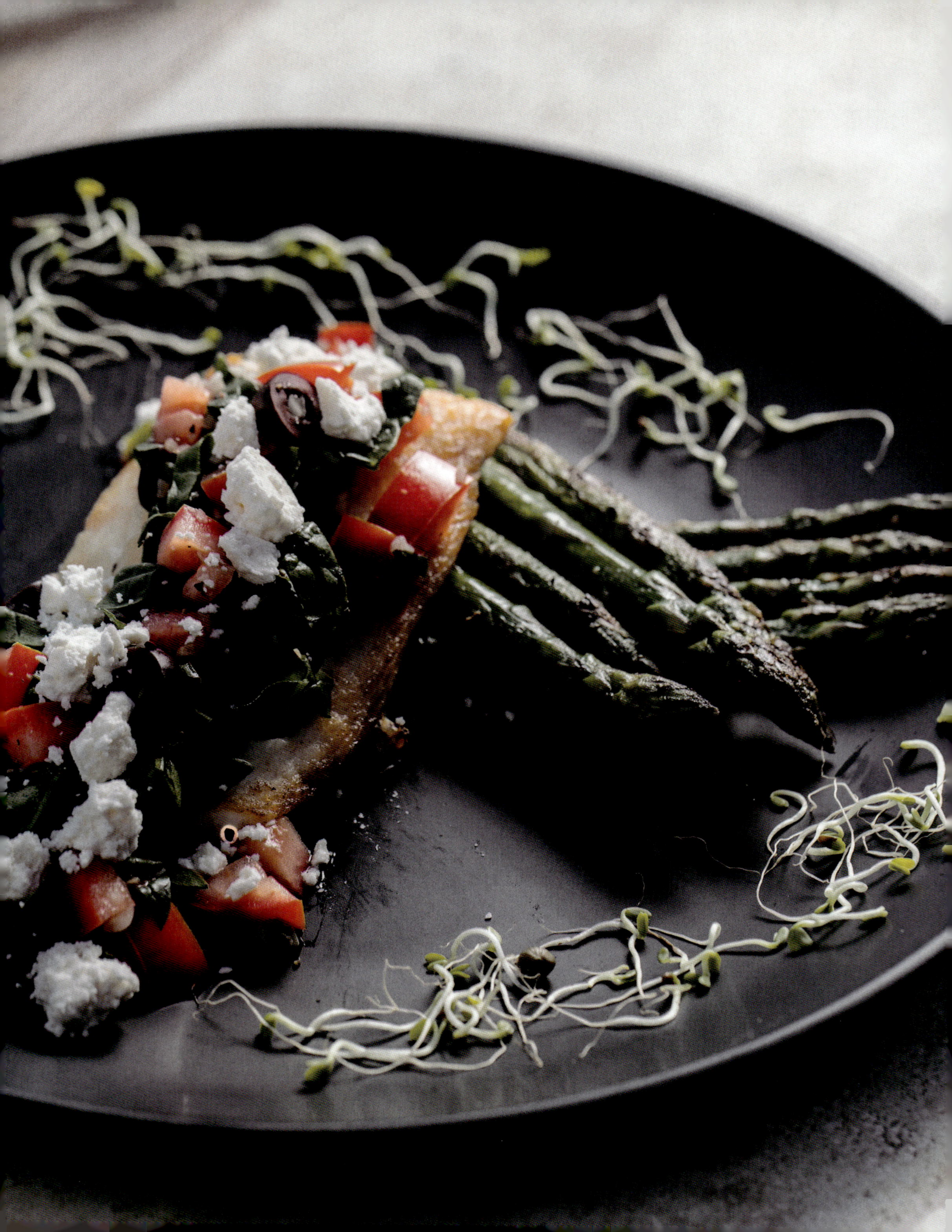

SERVING SIZE 2

FRESCO'S WATERFRONT DINING BISTRO

FRESCO FISH
MEDITERRANEAN AMERICAN RED SNAPPER OVER SAUTÉED GARLIC ASPARAGUS

Fresco's Waterfront Dining Bistro in downtown St. Pete offers a casual and relaxing atmosphere with a waterfront view of the Municipal Marina. The seafood-forward menu also serves salads, sandwiches and tacos, as well as gluten-free favorites like this one.

MEDITERRANEAN TOPPING
- 1 roma tomato, diced
- 6 kalamata green olives, chopped
- 1 tbsp capers
- 1 tsp garlic, minced
- 2 tbsp white wine
- ¼ cup olive oil
- ¼ cup spinach, chopped
- Juice of 1 lemon
- Salt and pepper to taste

FISH AND ASPARAGUS
- 12 ounces red snapper, separated into two filets
- 2 tsps garlic, minced
- 4 tbsp feta cheese
- 1 bunch asparagus

Mediterranean Topping
1. Add ingredients into small mixing bowl, salt and pepper to taste.
2. Set aside to marinade at room temperature.

Fish and Asparagus
1. Heat 2 medium pans to medium heat.
2. Add 2 tablespoons olive oil to one pan, followed by the two filets, cook for 5 minutes.
3. Flip and cover for an additional 5 minutes. Once complete, turn off heat and leave covered until serving.
4. While the fish cooks, in the second pan, add remaining olive oil, garlic, and asparagus and cook for 2 minutes.
5. Turn off heat and cover.
6. Add salt and pepper to taste.
7. Plate dishes with asparagus, followed by red snapper, and top with Mediterranean mixture and feta cheese.

SERVING SIZE 4

THE FLORIBBEAN

TROPICAL TAILS
CITRUS POACHED GULF SHRIMP, CILANTRO PISTOU WITH TOASTED TROPICAL QUINOA SALAD

CILANTRO PISTOU
2 ounces cilantro
1 ounce of basil
¼ tsp red chili flake
1 tsp salt
¼ tsp black pepper
2 ounces extra virgin olive oil
1 ounce key lime juice
1 ¼ tsp garlic cloves

QUINOA SALAD
1 cup rinsed quinoa
2 ½ cups water
5 ounces diced mango
4 ounces diced roasted red pepper
4 ounces diced red onion
2 tbsp olive oil
½ ounce honey
2 ounces lime juice
½ ounce kosher salt
3 grams black pepper
½ ounce chopped cilantro

SHRIMP
12 peeled and deveined wild gulf shrimp
6 ounces chopped sweet onion
2 qts. water
½ ounce kosher salt
1 ½ tsp black peppercorns
¾ tsp allspice berries
1 medium bay leaf
1 tbsp salt
4 ounces Florida oranges
2 ounces lime
2 ounces lemon
1 ounce cilantro stems
1 ounce of garlic cloves

One of the younger concepts on the food scene, **The Floribbean**, is a fast-casual restaurant featuring cuisine inspired by Caribbean and Florida classics as well as French, Latin, Creole and Asian flavors. This recipe includes components from the local gulf waters, as well as citrus and honey. This guilt-free dish provides robust flavor to satisfy discerning palates.

Quinoa Salad
1. Gather and measure all ingredients before beginning.
2. In a 2 quart stock pot add the water and quinoa.
3. Bring the quinoa to a simmer and cook until the water evaporates.
4. Take the pot off the heat and cover to steam for 5 minutes.
5. Spread the cooked quinoa on a sheet pan and cool.
6. Once the quinoa is cool, add in the diced mango, onion and roasted red pepper; stir to incorporate.
7. Add the oil, honey, and remaining ingredients, mix well.
8. Refrigerate.

Cilantro Pistou
1. Gather and measure all ingredients before beginning.
2. In a food processor, add olive oil first, then add the remaining ingredients.
3. Pulse the ingredients to begin to incorporate. Once it begins to incorporate, start to process fully until smooth.
4. Set aside.

Shrimp Preperation

1. In a 1 gallon stock pot, add all ingredients and bring to a simmer.
2. Reduce heat to until the water is 160 degrees.
3. Add peeled and deveined shrimp and turn off the heat to the stove.
4. Cook until shrimp they begin to turn opaque (keep an eye on these, it won't take long at all).
5. Once opaque, remove the shrimp from the poaching liquid and lay out on a sheet tray to cool.
6. Once the shrimp is cooled, toss the shrimp with the cilantro pistou.
7. Place coated shrimp ontop of quinoa salad and serve.

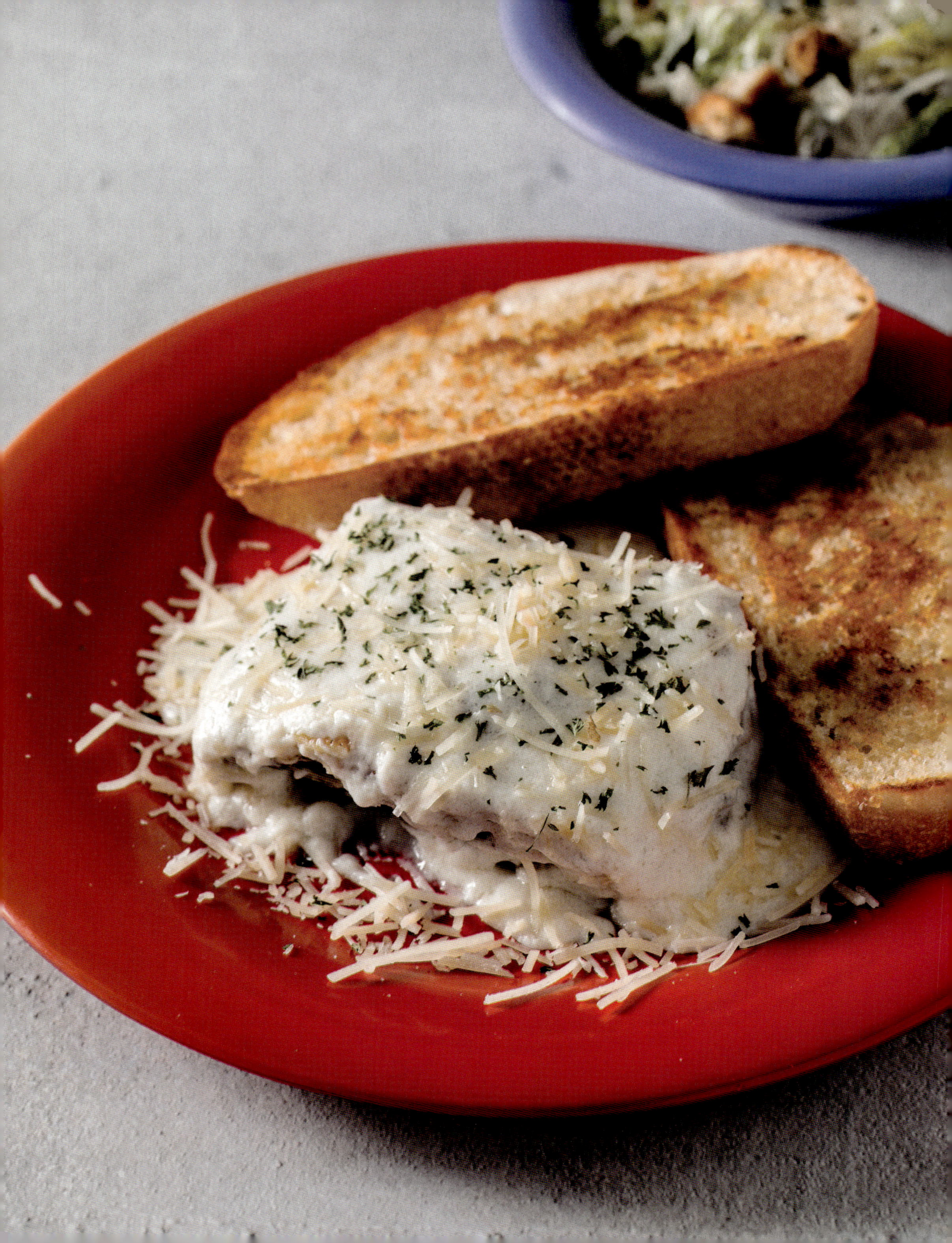

SERVING SIZE 9

PUNKY'S BAR AND GRILL

VEGGIE LASAGNA
WITH HOMEMADE ALFREDO SAUCE

Lasagna noodles
Spinach
Mushrooms
Provolone cheese

ALFREDO SAUCE
1 lb. butter
1 cup flour
1 ½ cups whole milk, plus extra as needed
1 ½ cup parmesan cheese
Salt and pepper, to taste

Punky's Bar and Grill is a highly decorated restaurant, featuring a slew of awards from local publications for brunch, late-night offerings, bingo and Best LGBTQ Club/Bar.

1. Preheat oven 450 degrees.
2. Prepare lasagna noodles by bringing salted water to a boil in a large stock pot. Cook lasagna noodles until al dente 8 to 10 minutes; check box for al dente cook time. Once noodles are cooked, strain noodles and place in large bowl filled with cold water. Set aside until lasagna assembly.
3. Prepare alfredo sauce by combining butter, flour, milk, and parmesan in a medium sauce pan over medium heat until combine. Season with salt and pepper.
4. In baking dish, layer noodles, spinach, mushrooms, provolone cheese, and alfredo sauce.
5. Cover with foil and cook for 40 minutes, uncover and cook an additional 15 minutes.
6. Serve with alfredo sauce on top.

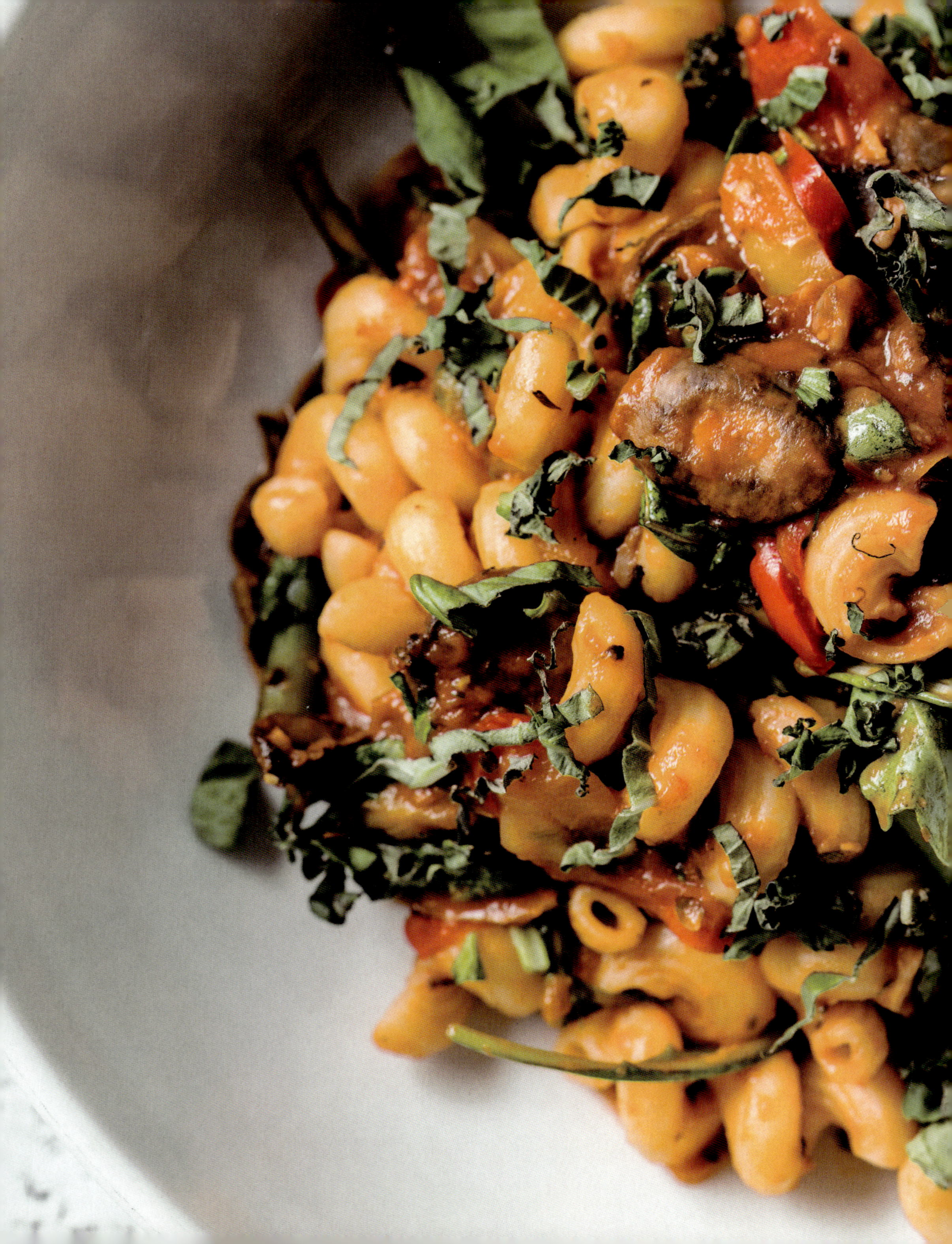

SERVING SIZE 1-2

BELLABRAVA NEW WORLD TRATTORIA

PASTA ARRABBIATA
SERVED WITH CHOPPED BROCCOLINI

- **4 ounces broccolini, chopped**
- **4 ounces mushrooms**
- **2 ounces grape tomatoes, halved**
- **1 tbsp olive oil**
- **6 garlic cloves, minced**
- **2 cups Chardonnay**
- **8 ounces marinara sauce**
- **2 tsps chili flakes**
- **16 ounces dry pasta**
- **Salt and pepper to taste**
- **Chiffonade basil, for garnish**

BellaBrava New World Trattoria is where vineyard-lined dreams come alive. Embraced by Downtown St. Pete since opening in 2005, BellaBrava showcases old-world flavor mingling with new-world flair. Whether sampling seafood or famous American burgers with a Tuscan twist, the Italian mainstay has something the entire family can enjoy.

1. Oven roast mushrooms and grape tomatoes for 12 minutes at 400 degrees. Set aside.
2. Blanch broccolini for 90 seconds in boiling water. Remove and place into ice water until cold.
3. Begin sauce in a medium stock pot on medium-high heat by adding olive oil to coat the entire bottom surface.
4. Add broccolini cook for 10 minutes.
5. Add garlic, cook until golden brown.
6. Add chili flakes and wine.
7. Reduce contents by half.
8. Add marinara.
9. Reduce heat to medium and simmer for 20 minutes.
10. Cook pasta according to box directions while sauce is simmering.
11. Once pasta is cooked, strain and add directly into pot.
12. Salt and pepper to taste.
13. Garnish with chiffonade basil.

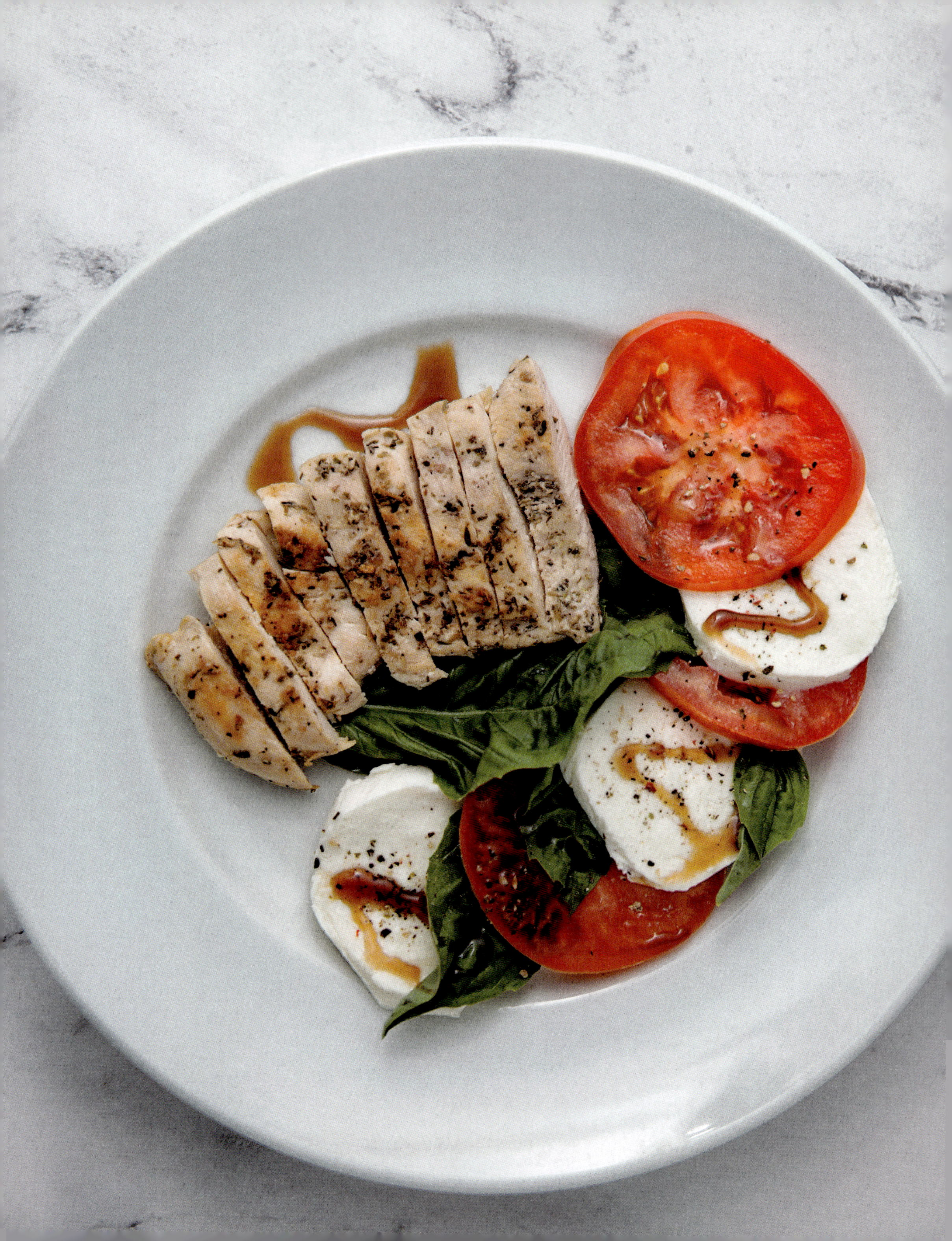

SERVING SIZE 4

DR. KANIKA TOMALIN'S CLASSIC CAPRESE WITH CHICKEN

WITH FRESH MOZZARELLA AND GARDEN-RIPE TOMATOES

2 chicken breasts
Olive oil
Italian seasonings
Salt and pepper
Fresh mozzarella, sliced into ½ inch pieces
2 large tomatoes, sliced into ½ inch pieces
Reduced balsamic vinegar
Fresh basil

So many mouths to feed... My kids. My kids' friends. My friends who drop by. My family who might show up any minute. Around my house, I have to be ready at any time to create a healthy meal that takes no time. This delicious, quick-to-fix dish is one of my favorites.

1. Coat the bottom of a medium-sized frying pan with light olive oil.
2. Season chicken with your favorite Italian seasoning, or lightly with salt and pepper.
3. Brown chicken over medium heat until both sides are golden brown. Remove from heat.
4. Pick and clean basil, separating from stem into individual leaves about the same size of cheese.
5. Arrange one piece of mozzarella, basil, and tomato in repeating order on each plate that is to be served. Slice chicken into thin strips and fan alongside salad. Drizzle with olive oil and balsamic vinegar. Sprinkle with salt and pepper to taste.

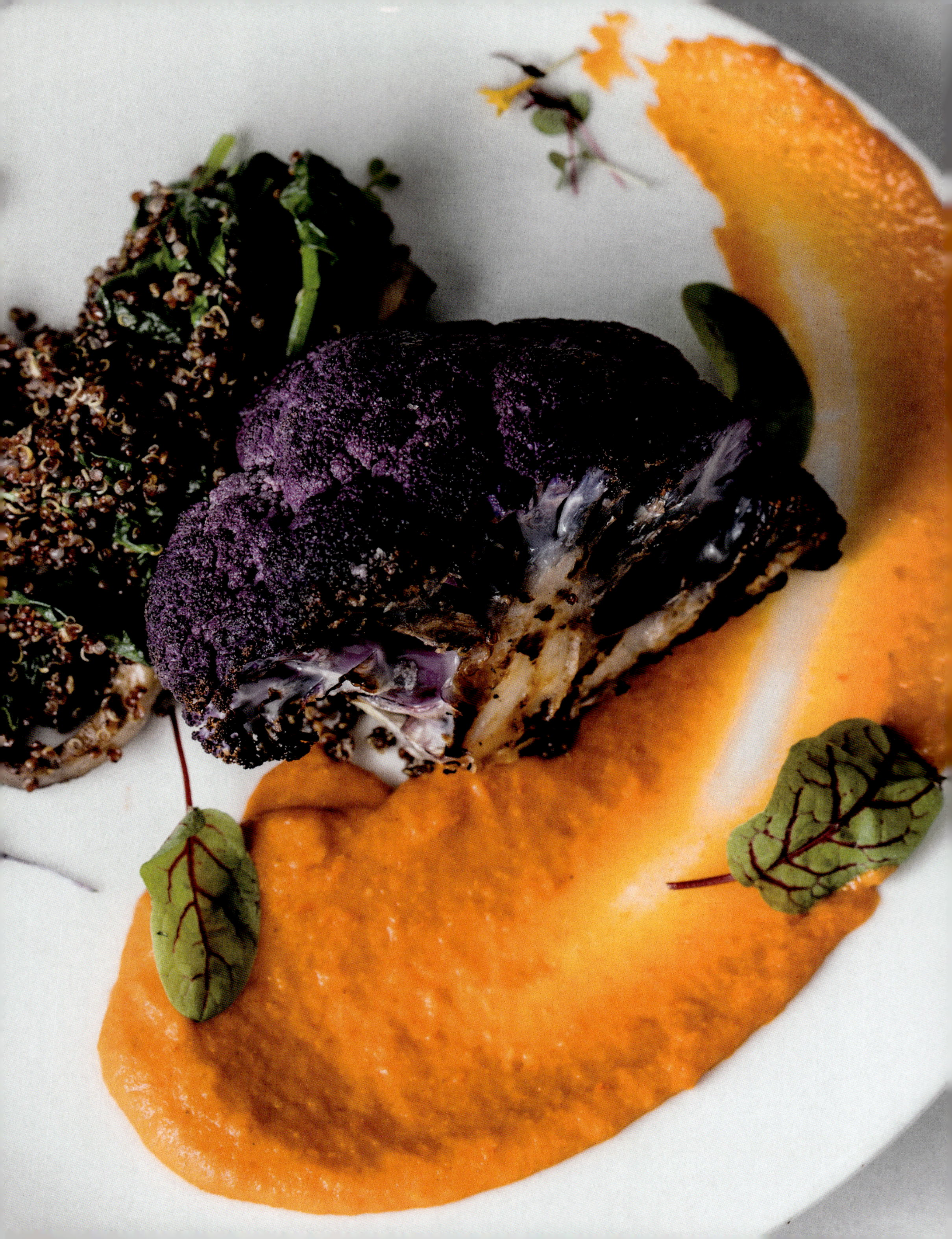

SERVING SIZE 8

THE LIBRARY

CAULIFLOWER STEAK
WITH ROMESECO SAUCE AND QUINOA

ROMESCO SAUCE
2 large red peppers, deseeded and chopped
4 roma tomatoes, chopped
¼ cup of toasted almonds
2 garlic cloves
¼ white onion, chopped
¼ teaspoon smoked paprika
¼ tbsp red wine vinegar
½ tbsp salt and pepper
2 tbsp olive oil
½ cup medium diced toasted white bread
Pinch of cayenne

ROASTED CAULIFLOWER
4 heads of purple or regular cauliflower
2 cups olive oil
Salt and pepper to taste

QUINOA
4 cup cooked quinoa
4 tbsp minced garlic
1 tbsp minced shallot
4 tbsp olive oil
8 cup spinach
6 portobello mushrooms, chopped

The Library, located on the Johns Hopkins All Children's Hospital campus, offers a menu curated by James Beard semifinalist Chef Rachel Bennett.

Romesco Sauce
1. Toss red peppers, roma tomatoes, garlic cloves, and white onion in olive oil, salt, and pepper.
2. Roast at 375 degrees for 25 minutes.
3. Blend roasted vegetables in a blender with almonds and bread until completely smooth.
4. Transfer to a bowl and whisk with the spices and vinegar.

Roasted Cauliflower
1. Cut stem off cauliflower and cut in half. Toss in olive oil and sprinkle with salt and pepper.
2. Place on a baking sheet and cover with aluminum foil.
3. Roast at 375 degrees for 25 minutes until fork tender.
4. Toss on grill or cast iron skillet, flat side down to get a nice char.

Quinoa
1. In a large pan, sauté all ingredients.
2. Add salt and pepper to taste.

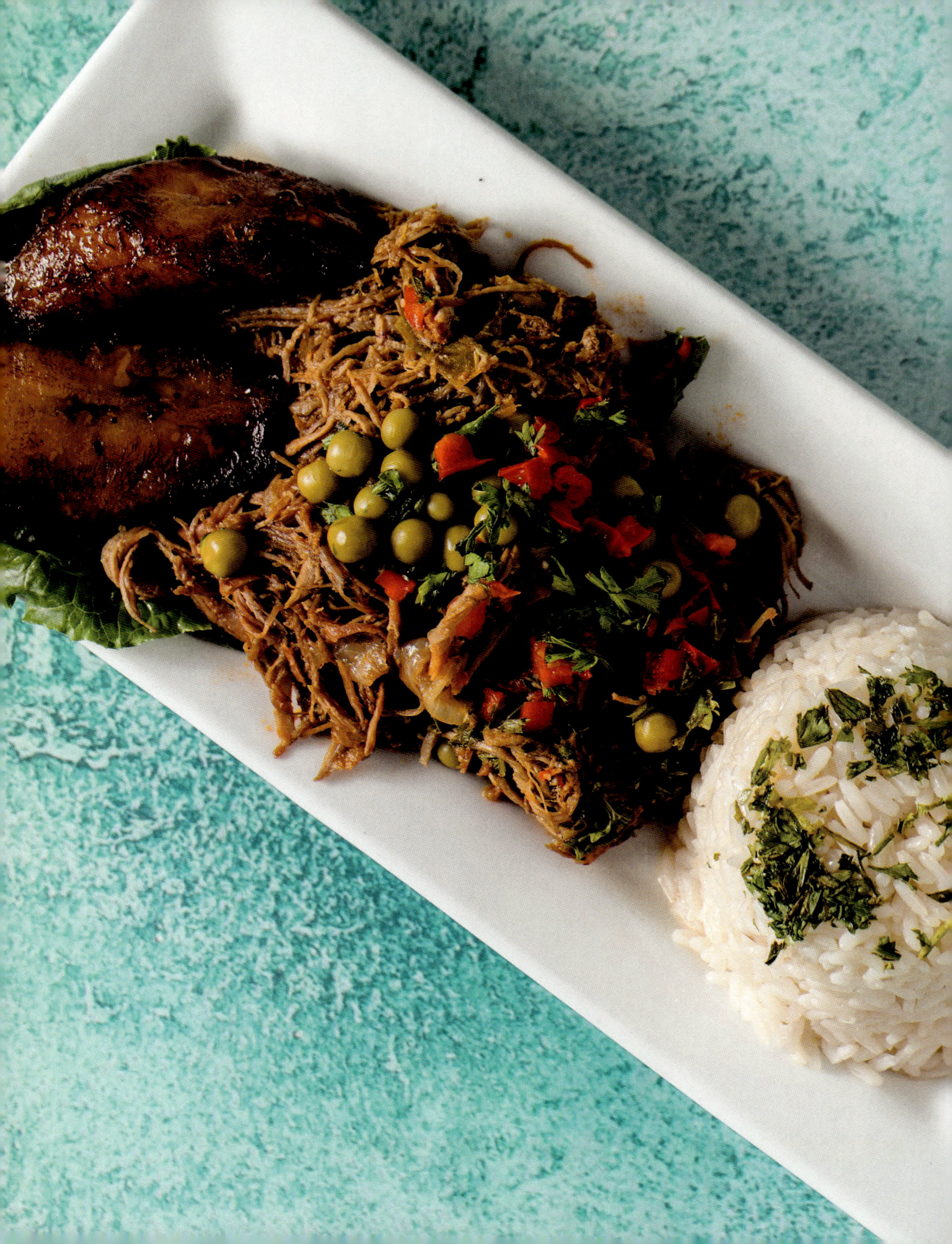

SERVING SIZE 10

PIPO'S CUBAN CAFE

ROPA VIEJA
SHREDDED FLANK STEAK SERVED OVER RICE

Flank steak
4 bell peppers, cut in strips
2 Spanish onions, cut in strips
2 tomatoes, chopped
¼ cup cilantro, chopped
1 tbsp oregano leaf
1 tbsp ground cumin
2 tbsp garlic, chopped
½ tbsp sugar
1 tsp salt, add more to taste
½ cup tomato paste
2 tbsp Spanish paprika
1 cup red wine
¼ cup olive oil
Cooked white rice

More than three decades ago, The Hernandez family opened their first *Pipo's Cuban Cafe* in Tampa Bay. Focused on staying true to the tradition and authentic flavors of Cuban cuisine, they committed to use only quality ingredients and proven family recipes to build their menu. Whether you choose the award-winning roast pork, the mouth-watering black beans and Spanish rice, or a rich Cuban espresso, you are guaranteed to experience the vibrant, diverse flavors and aromas of authentic Cuban cuisine.

1. Place flank steak in boiling water till tender, approximately 2 hours.
2. Remove and shred meat when cool. Do not discard beef broth.
3. In a braising pan over medium heat, add oil, onions, peppers, tomatoes, cilantro, and garlic lightly sauté veggies.
4. Add all spices, wine, and tomato paste. Stir until mixture thickens.
5. Add shredded beef and 3 to 4 cups of beef broth.
6. Mix well, bring to a boil then turn temperature to low and let it simmer for 30 minutes.
7. Serve over rice.

SERVING SIZE 4

1 head romaine lettuce, quartered
1 ounce cilantro
8 ounces cilantro vinaigrette (recipe follows)
4 ounces pumpkin seeds

QUINOA
1 cup red quinoa (tricolor quinoa can also be substituted)
2 cups water
½ tbsp kosher salt

GREEN CHILI CREMA
1 ¼ lbs. sour cream
¼ cup chili pepper, diced
¼ tsp kosher salt
¼ tbsp lime juice
¼ cup buttermilk

CILANTRO VINAIGRETTE DRESSING
1 cup green onion, chopped
1 ¼ bunches cilantro, leaves only
2 cups rice wine vinegar
1 cup lime juice
¼ tbsp ground black pepper
¼ tbsp kosher salt
2 cups olive oil
1 tbsp wildflower honey

CHARRED VEGGIES
8 ounces baby carrots
8 ounces brussel sprouts, shaved
8 ounces red onion, julienned
8 ounces red bell pepper, cut into ¼ inch strips
8 ounces golden beets, pre-cooked
8 ounces button mushrooms, sliced
1 cup vegetable oil
1 tsp kosher salt
½ tbsp ground pepper

THE CANYON CAFÉ

BUDDHA BOWL
SALAD BOWL WITH QUINOA AND GREEN CHILI CREMA

Nestled in The James Museum of Western & Wildlife Art, ***The Canyon Café*** lets diners enjoy a meal as colorful and artistic as the exhibits. The Canyon features shareables, sandwiches, bowls and salads for visitors to enjoy dining in or grabbing a bite to go.

Quinoa
1. Place water and salt in a medium pot and bring to a boil.
2. Add quinoa and reduce to a simmer.
3. Cook for 12 to 15 minutes, remove from heat and cover to rest.
4. Drain any remaining liquid and cool.

Green Chili Crema
1. Purée chilis.
2. Combine all ingredients into mixing bowl and whisk until well blended.
3. Cover and refrigerate.

Cilantro Vinaigrette Dressing
1. Combine all ingredients (except honey).
2. Blend with immersion blender or high speed blender until smooth.
3. Slowly stream in honey while blending.
4. Cover and refrigerate.

Charred Veggies
1. Preheat oven to 350 degrees.
2. In a large mixing bowl, combine all ingredients and mix well. Place a piece of parchment paper on a sheet pan and pull out just carrots and roast for 15 minutes.
3. Remove pan from oven an add remaining vegetables and place back in oven for an additional 20 minutes.
4. Veggies are best served slightly warm or at room temperature.

Assembly

1. Divide quinoa evenly into 4 bowls and microwave for 1 minute.
2. Place charred vegetables into preheated 350 degree oven for 10 minutes until warmed through.
3. In a mixing bowl, toss romaine in with 4 ounces of cilantro vinaigrette, covering all leaves evenly, then place a romaine wedge on one side of each bowl.
4. Remove charred vegetables from oven and toss with remaining 4 ounces of cilantro vinaigrette and place equal amounts of vegetables on opposite side of bowl.
5. In a zig zag pattern, drizzle lime crema over vegetables.
6. Top lettuce with pumpkin seeds.

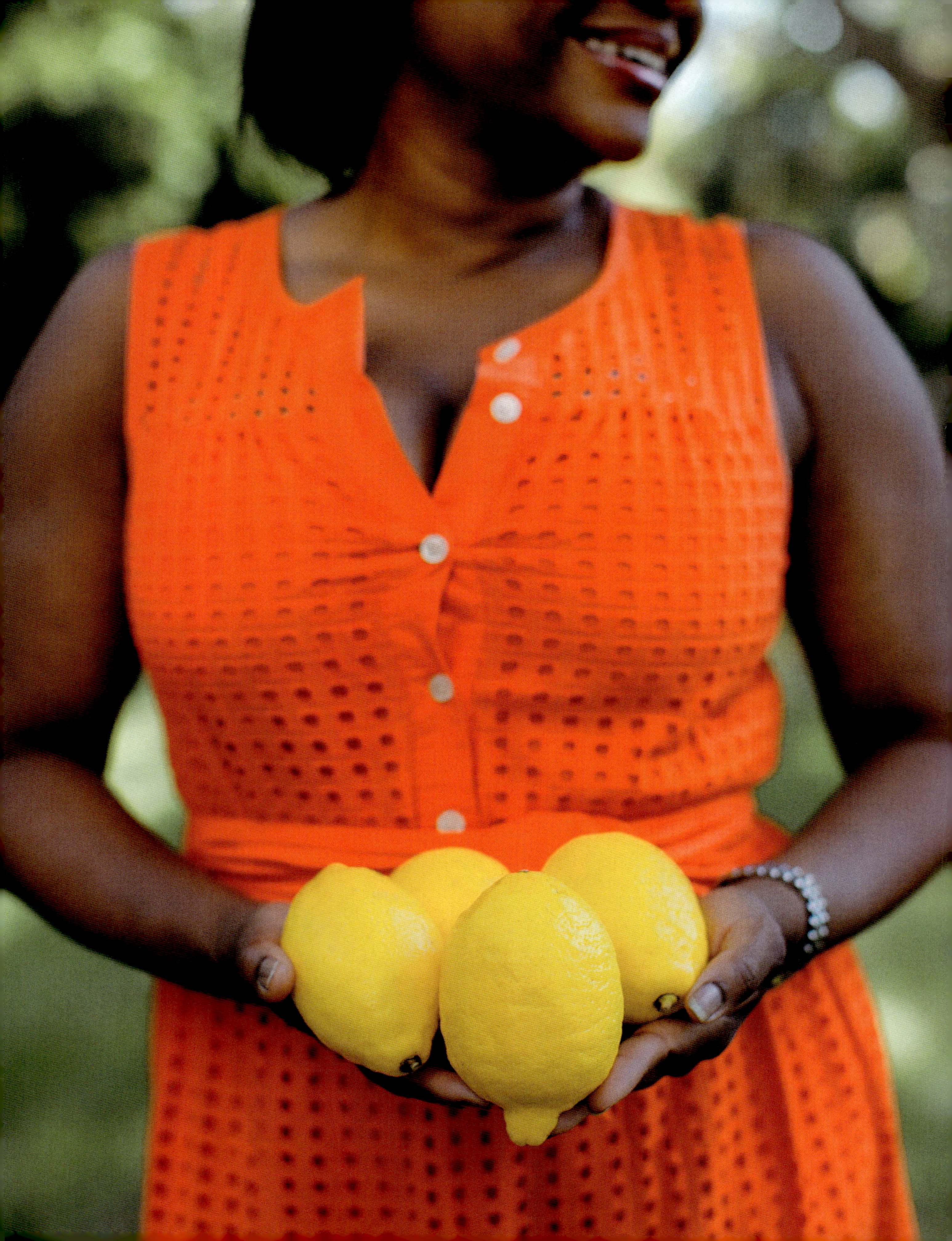

> *...cooking is an expression of love, creating memories that will last a lifetime.*

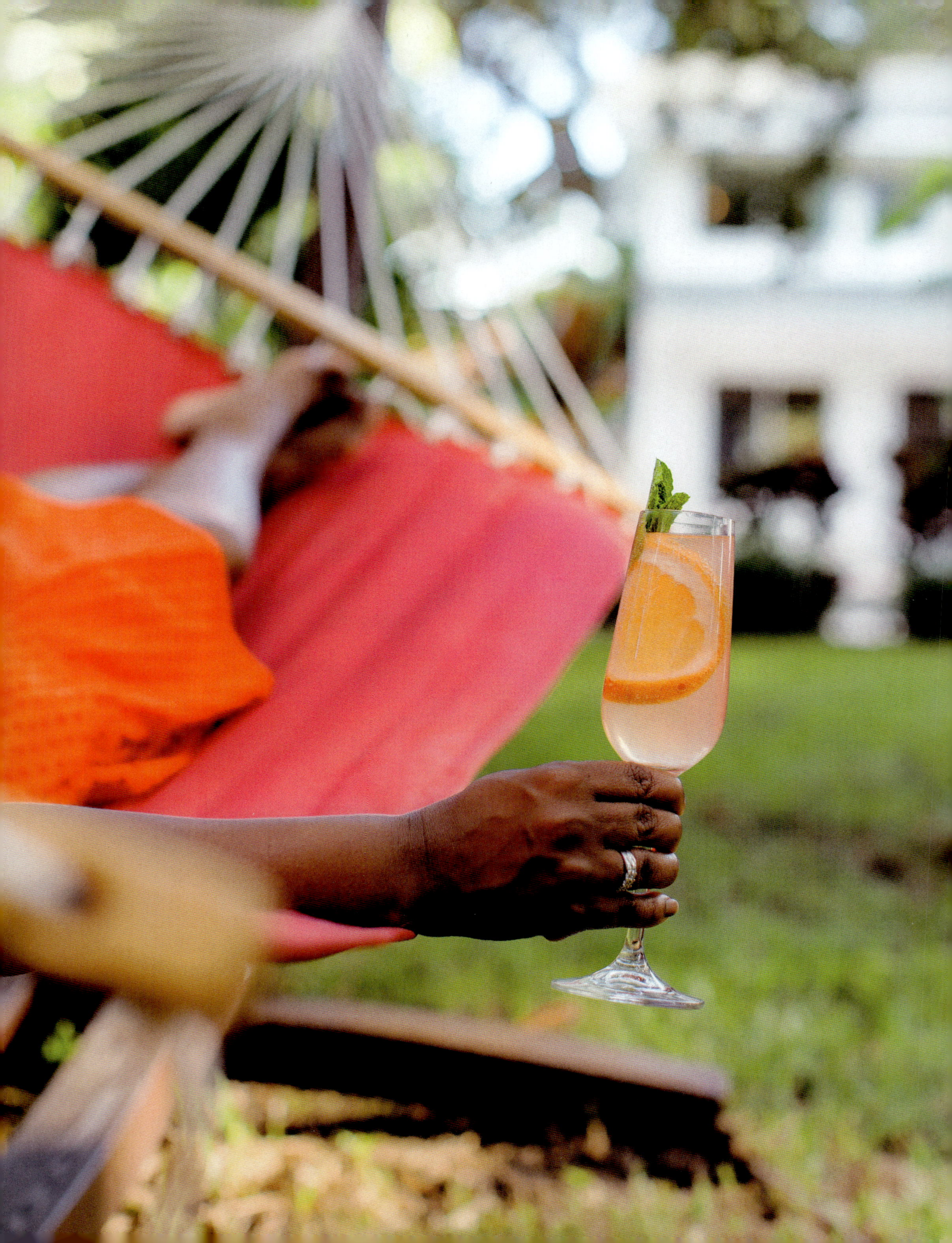

- CHAPTER 4 -
COCKTAILS

A cocktail can be versatile, evolving with the seasons. The choice is yours, but of course, moderation is key. A mixed drink is typically less filling than beer, and can be an added layer to your presentation. Local bars and restaurants have shared the skill of their crafty mixologists to create cocktail recipes that will wow. These sips can be enjoyed after a long day at work, a start to your date night, or even a night cap at your dinner party. Get creative with your flair, make them as strong or as subtle as you please. These recipes are yours to recreate and enjoy.

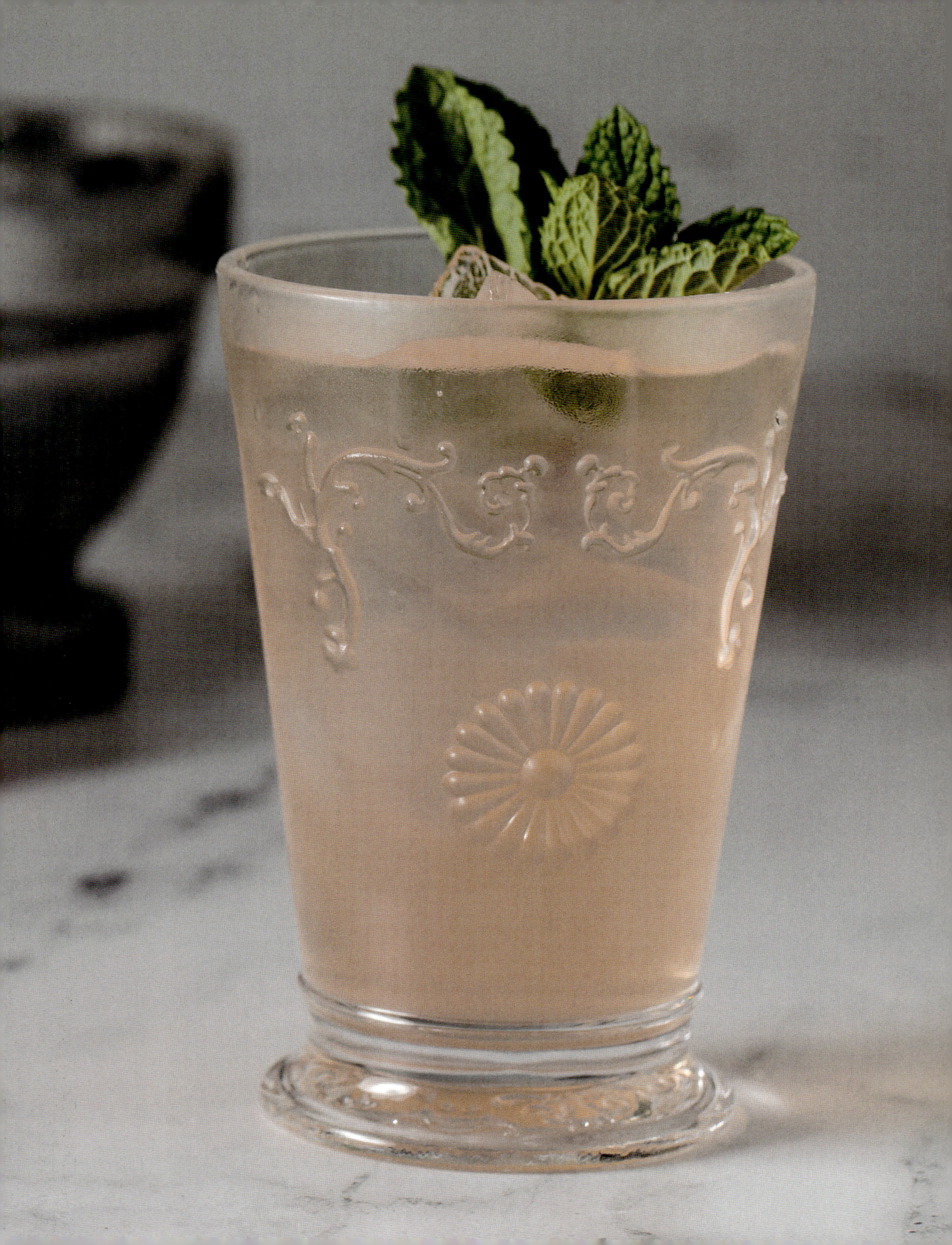

109	SUGAR-FREE SIPS
111	MATCHA MADE IN HEAVEN
113	THYME AFTER TIME
115	THE AVIATOR
117	STRAWBERRY MINT JULEP
119	HEMINGWAY DAIQUIRI
121	SAN SABA SONGBIRD
123	HEMP DAY
125	DR. KANIKA TOMALIN'S BE PREPARED

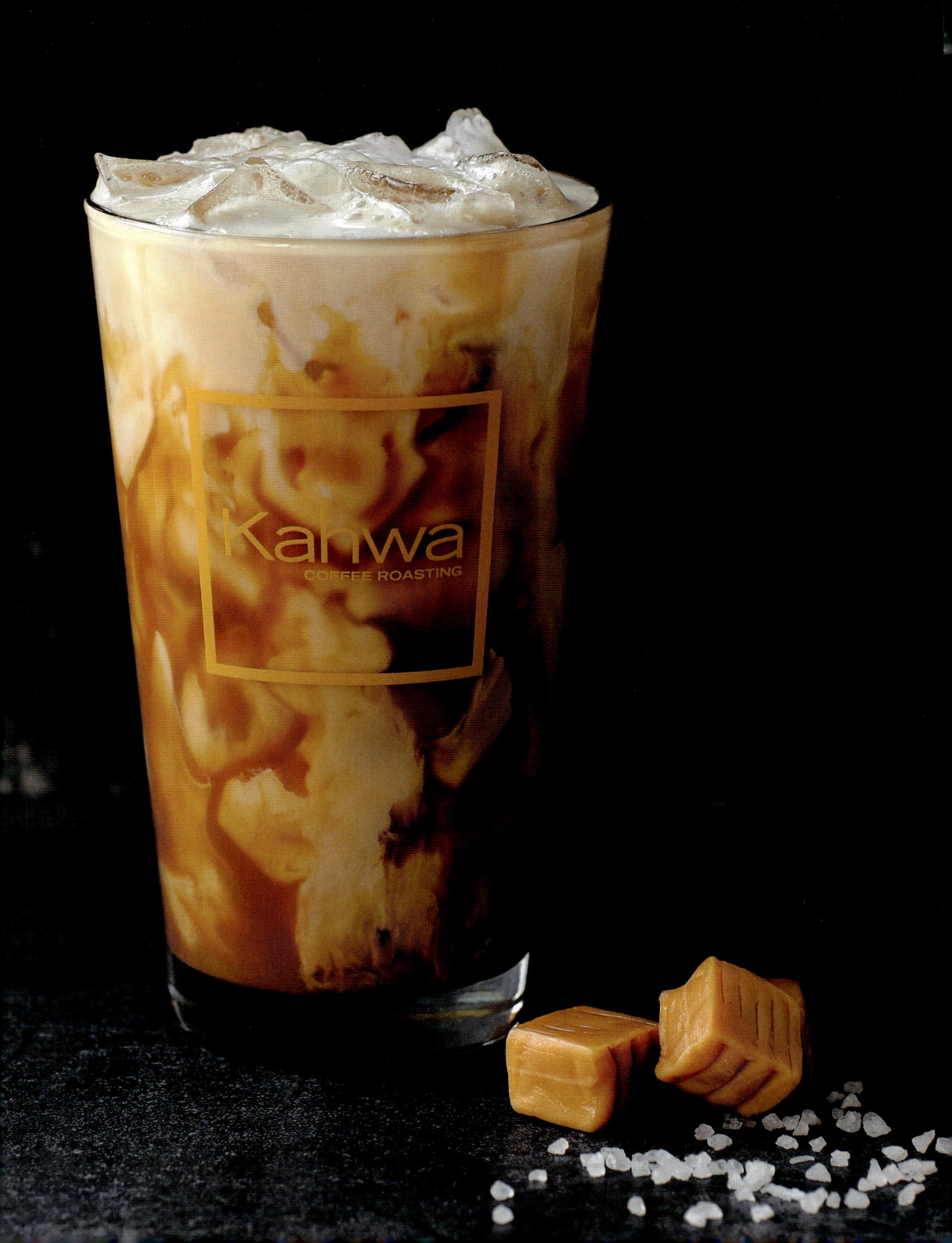
Kahwa
COFFEE ROASTING

SERVING SIZE 1

KAHWA

SUGAR-FREE SIPS
SUGAR-FREE SALTED CARAMEL COLD BREW

1 cup Kahwa Coffee Cold Brew
2 pumps of Jordan's Skinny Syrups sugar-free salted caramel syrup, or your preferred store-bought sugar-free flavored syrup
Almond milk

Kahwa is a St. Pete-born coffee shop chain specializing in locally-roasted coffee and delicious breakfast and pastry items. This drink is prime for an after-dinner pick-me-up. Gluten-free, vegan and with enough caffeine to boost you through dessert or that after-meal conversation.

1. Combine cold brew and caramel syrup.
2. Add preferred amount of almond milk to taste.
3. Serve over ice.

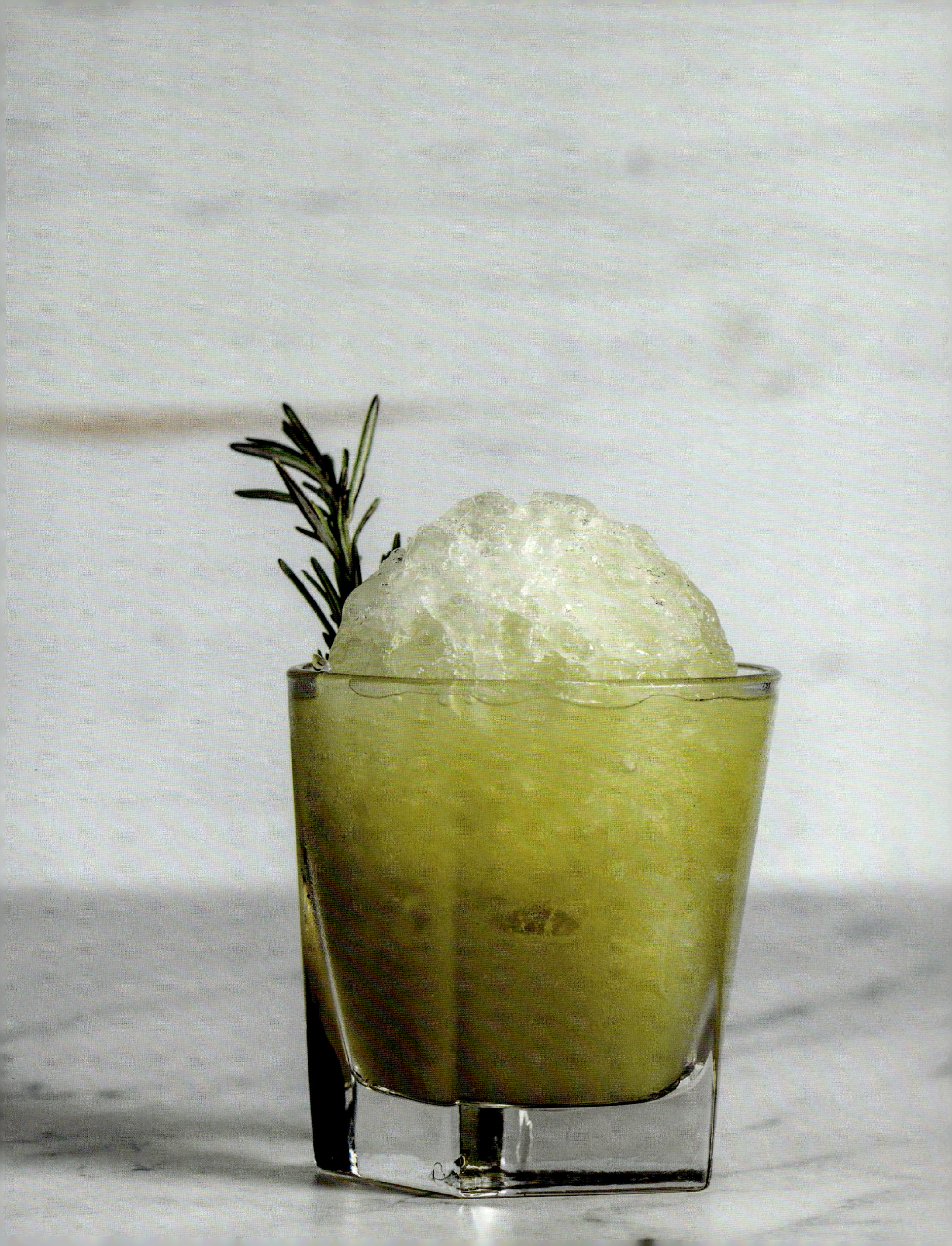

SERVING SIZE 4

MANDARIN HIDE

MATCHA MADE IN HEAVEN
MOCKTAIL WITH FRESH LEMONGRASS TO GARNISH

- 1 can (13.5 ounces) coconut milk
- 2 tbsp matcha green tea powder
- 2 ounces agave syrup
- ¼ cup fresh lemongrass
- 2 ounces fresh lemon juice
- Carbonated mineral water
- Fresh lemongrass to garnish

The steward of craft cocktail culture, **Mandarin Hide**, aims to find the perfect drink for each guest's preferences. In addition to carrying one of the largest inventories of spirits, Mandarin Hide also offers a bevy of craft beers and excellent wines. The cocktail lodge is truly pouring spirits to raise yours. If you choose to spike this matcha mocktail, add your preferred spirit to the first step of the recipe. Or simply sip and enjoy this refreshing, guilt-free mocktail as-is.

1. Blend the coconut milk, matcha powder, agave syrup, lemongrass, and lemon juice in a high-speed blender.
2. Strain into a collins glass over crushed ice.
3. Top with a splash of mineral water.
4. Garnish with a piece of fresh lemongrass.

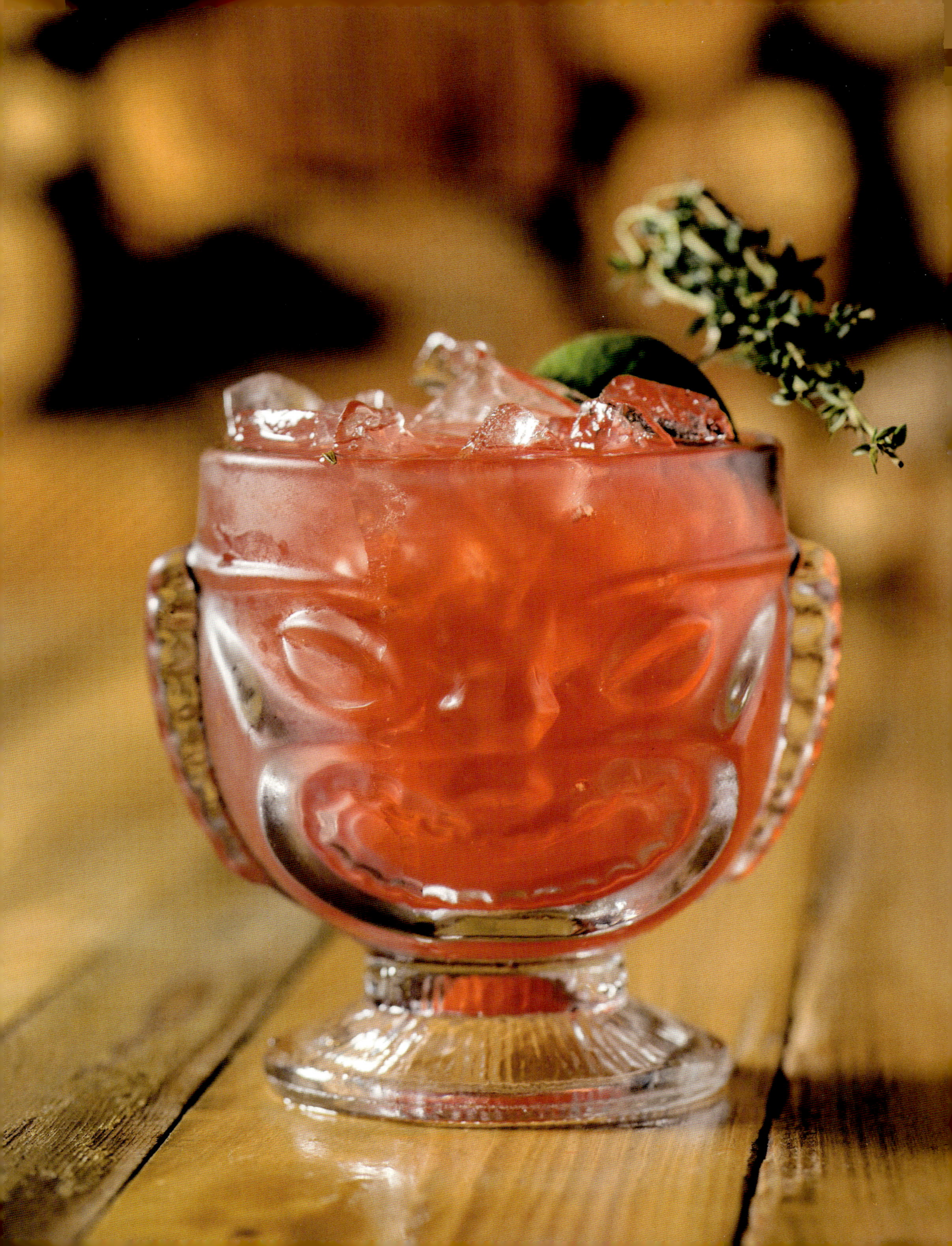

SERVING SIZE 1

THE LURE

THYME AFTER TIME
TEQUILA COCKTAIL WITH THYME SPRIG AND LIME

- 2 ounces thyme-infused Corazon Reposado Tequila
- 1 ounce fresh lime juice
- 1 ounce simple syrup
- 1 ounce Pama Pomegranate Liqueur
- Thyme sprig and lime slices, for garnish

The Lure has created an experience with extraordinary sushi, mouthwatering tapas, tacos and flatbreads. These delights are accompanied by potent tikis and award-winning local brews that make this spot a fun, friendly and laid-back atmosphere with five-star taste and service.

1. Grab a bottle of Corazon Reposado Tequila.
2. Pour out two shots to create space in bottle.
3. Fill the bottle with sprigs of thyme.
4. Re-cap, turn bottle up and down a few times and let sit overnight.
5. Next day, combine remaining ingredients in a shaker, shake well.
6. Pour over ice.

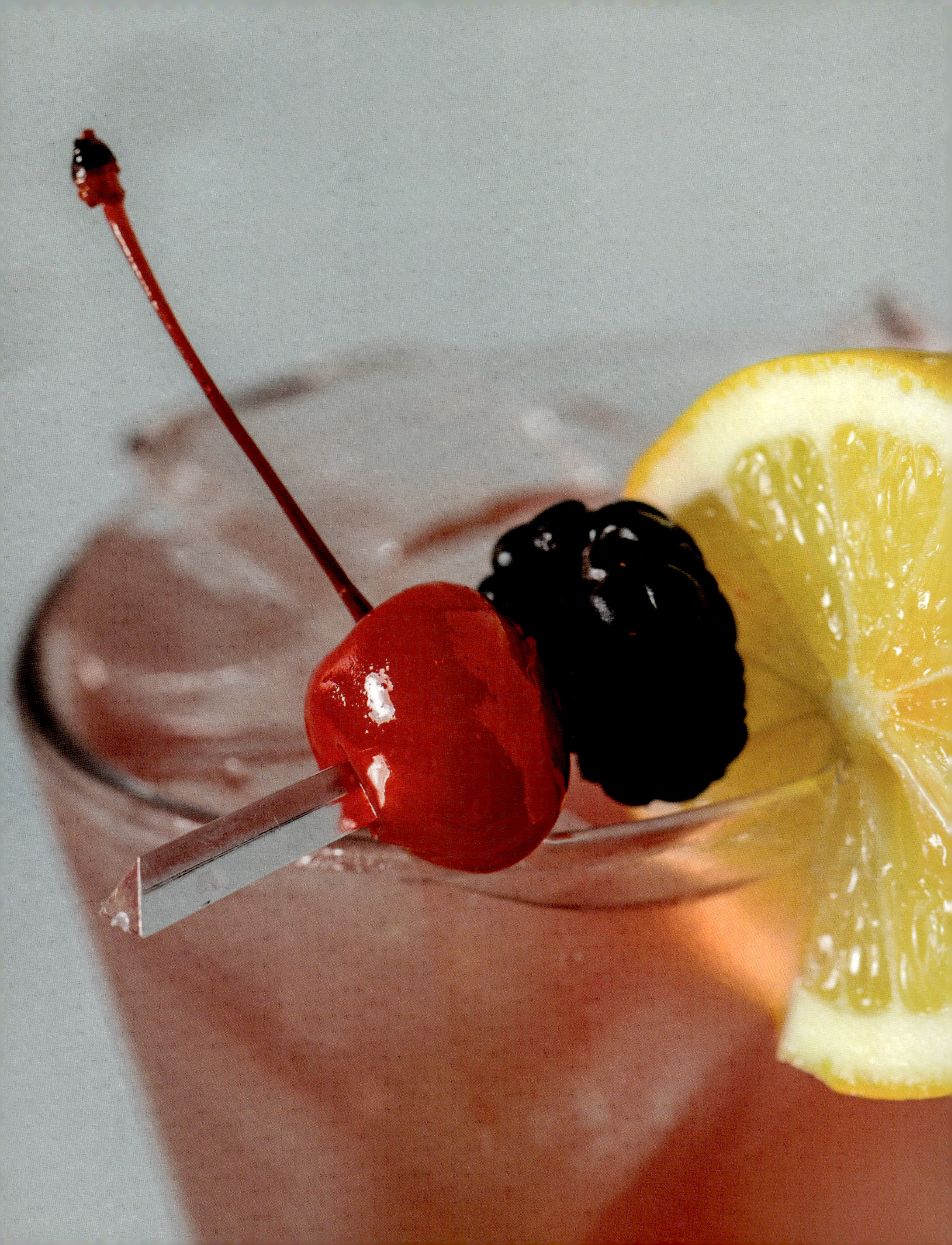

SERVING SIZE 1

FORD'S GARAGE ST. PETE

THE AVIATOR
GIN COCKTAIL WITH BLACK CHERRY PURÉE

2 ounces Aviation Gin
½ ounce black cherry purée
3 ounces lemonade
1 ½ ounces fresh soda water
Lemon wheels, maraschino cherries, and blackberries, for garnish.

Ford's Garage St. Pete is your top pit stop for delicious prime burgers, comfort food and delectable desserts in downtown St. Pete. The family-friendly atmosphere and fun decor make Ford's Garage an easy choice for a laid-back meal. All of these ingredients are suggestions, and can be replaced with spirits of your choice or whatever is readily available at home.

1. Place gin, black cherry purée and lemonade in shaker.
2. Dry shake.
3. Pour over ice in pint glass and top off with fresh soda water.
4. Garnish each glass with 1 lemon wheel, 1 maraschino cherry, and 1 blackberry.

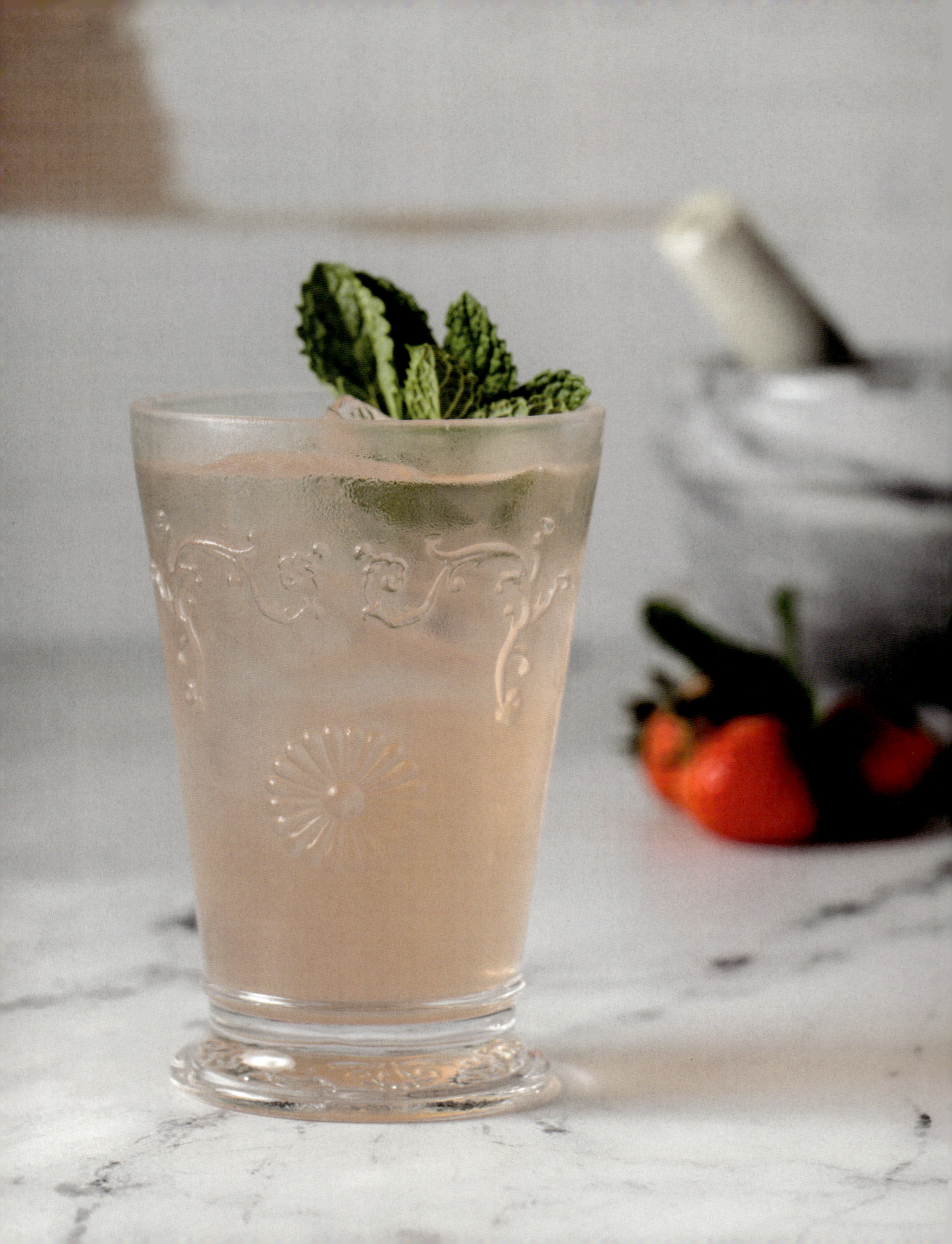

SERVING SIZE 2

TEBELLA TEA COMPANY

STRAWBERRY MINT JULEP MOCKTAIL
WITH MINT LEAF GARNISH

5 medium-sized strawberries, sliced
4 basil leaves, torn
6 mint leaves, torn
1 tbsp Mint Julep white tea
2 to 3 tsp of raw sugar or 1 tsp agave (personal preference)
Additional mint leaves for garnish

TeBella Tea Company shares this recipe as a refreshing option to a sweltering day in the 'Burg. The company has multiple locations around Tampa Bay and supplies tea to more than 100 cafes, restaurants, and hotels in the Southeast. An insider tip: if you choose to muddle ingredients by hand, it will release the aroma of the herbs better than simply puréeing in a food processor.

1. In a small to medium bowl (or using a mortar and pestle), muddle together the strawberries, basil, and mint until the strawberries release their juices and the mixture resembles a purée. Set aside.
2. Bring water to boil, then set aside for 1 minute.
3. In a measuring cup, add 1 tablespoon of Mint Julep loose tea, 2 tablespoons of the strawberry mixture, and preferred sweetener (if any).
4. Add 8 ounces of boiled water to the measuring cup and steep the tea with the strawberry mixture for 3 minutes.
5. Fill a cocktail shaker with ice.
6. When the tea is finished steeping, pour it into the cocktail shaker through a hand strainer.
7. Shake vigorously and then strain again into 2 glasses filled with ice.
8. Garnish with fresh mint.

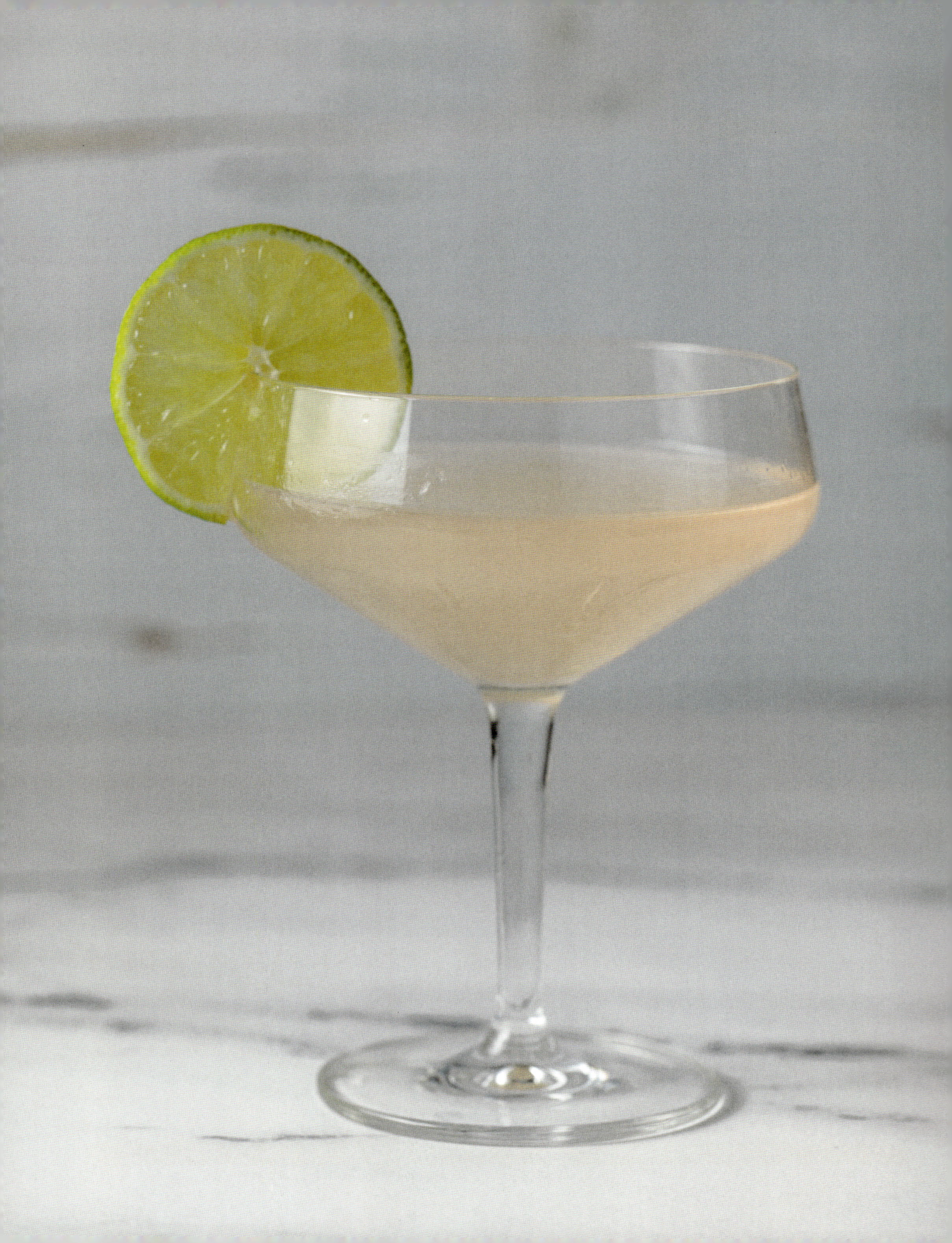

SERVING SIZE 1

THE LIBRARY

HEMINGWAY DAIQUIRI
WITH A LIME WHEEL GARNISH

2 ounces Don Q Cristal Rum
¼ ounce Luxardo Maraschino Liqueur
½ ounce fresh squeezed lime juice
½ ounce fresh squeezed grapefruit juice
¼ ounce simple syrup (add up to ½ ounce, if needed)
Lime wheel for garnish

The Library, located on the Johns Hopkins All Children's Hospital campus, offers a menu curated by James Beard semifinalist Chef Rachel Bennett. The Library is where the community as a whole comes to refill their cup, both proverbially and, often, quite literally. The ingredients for the Hemingway Daiquiri can be altered to fit your preference and what you have available. Keep in mind, the amount of simple syrup can depend on the sweetness of the fresh squeezed juices and personal preference.

1. Fill a cocktail shaker with ice.
2. Add the remaining ingredients and shake well.
3. Strain into a chilled coupe glass.
4. Garnish with the lime wheel.

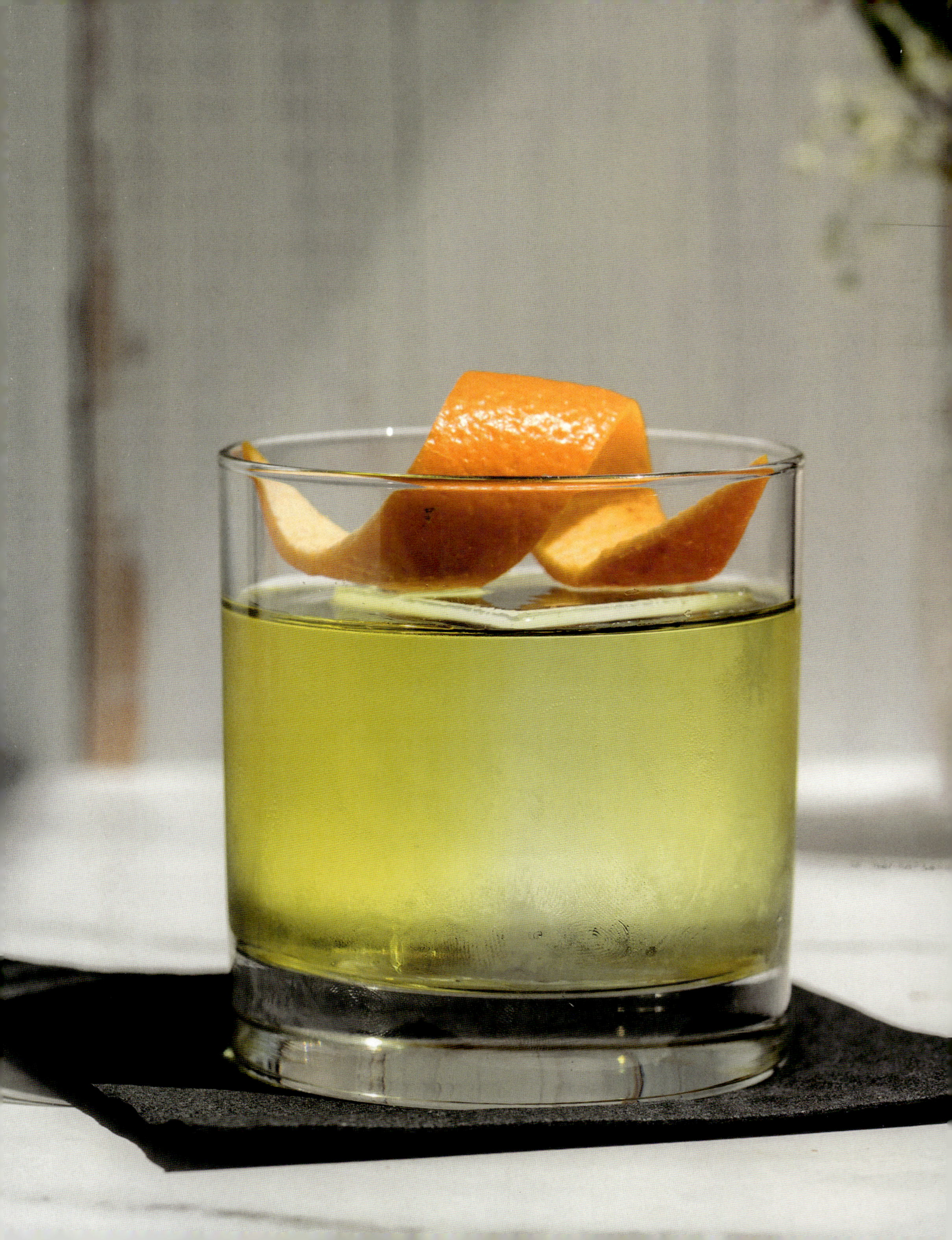

SERVING SIZE 4

INTERMEZZO

SAN SABA SONGBIRD

GIN COCKTAIL GARNISHED WITH LEMON PEEL

1 ounce St. George Botanivore Gin
¾ ounce Carpano Bianco Vermouth
¾ ounce Suze Liqueur
½ ounce Manzanilla Sherry
Lemon peel for garnish

Intermezzo is a specialty coffee shop and craft cocktail bar that provides a warm and friendly space for friends to gather over coffee, a bottle of wine or cocktails. Inspired by European and American cafés in the 1950s and 1960s, Intermezzo focuses on a balance in flavors, creating beverages that are both rooted in tradition and those that have modern, creative variation.

1. Combine ingredients into mixing glass, stir, and strain over a large ice cube.
2. Garnish with lemon peel.

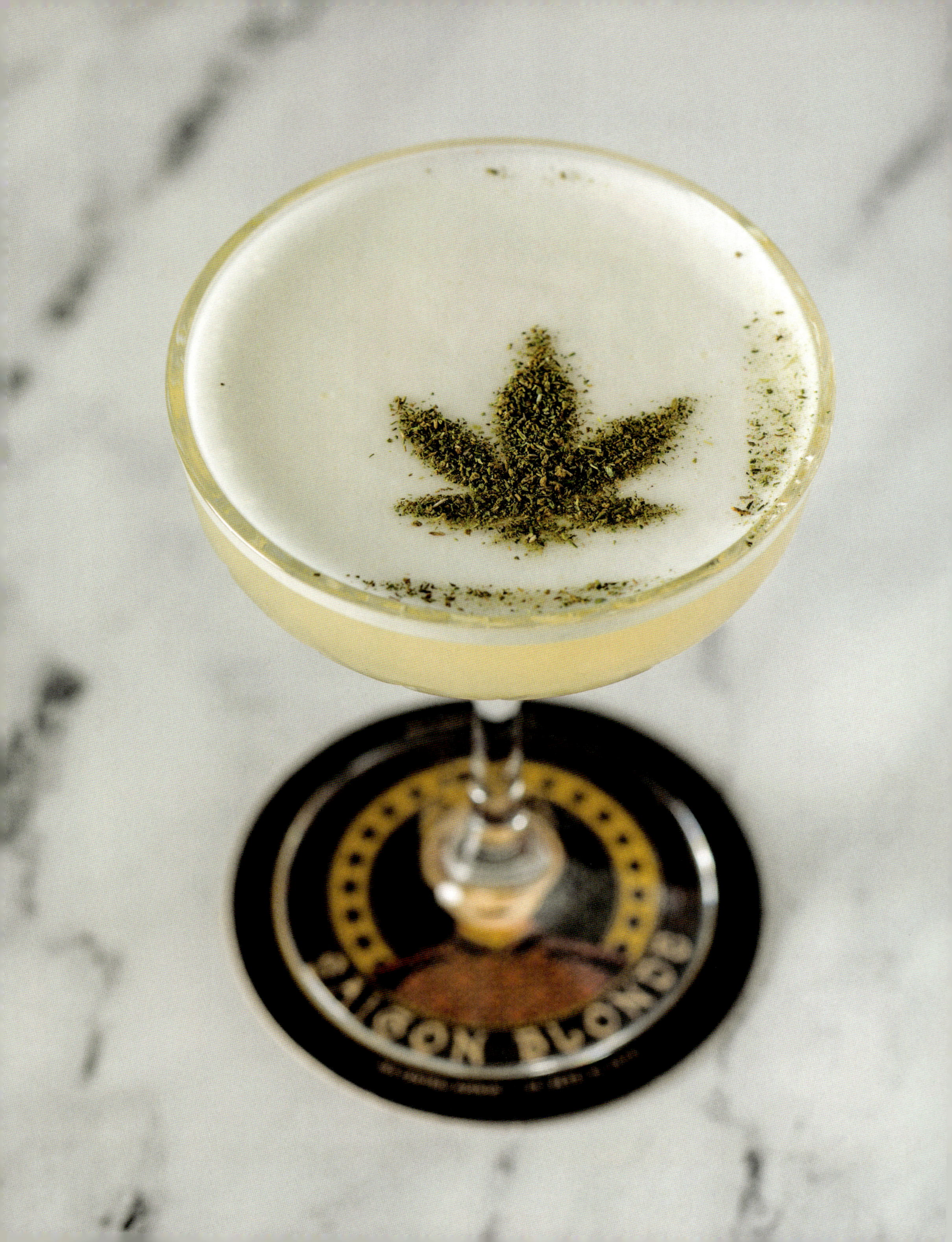
SAIGON BLONDE

SERVING SIZE 1

SAIGON BLONDE

HEMP DAY
VODKA COCKTAIL WITH POWDERED HEMP GARNISH

1 ½ ounces Banyan Reserve Vodka
¼ ounce jalapeño simple
¾ ounce fresh lime juice
¾ ounce orgeat
2 ounces SweetWater Brewery 420 Strain Mango Kush beer
Powdered hemp, for garnish

Saigon Blonde is a 1960s era-inspired tropical tiki lounge located on downtown St. Pete's bustling Central Avenue. All of these ingredients are suggested and can be replaced with your spirit of choice.

Jalapeño simple syrup
1. Boil 2 sliced jalapeños to a quart of simple syrup.
2. Add a few grinds of black pepper and 2 pinches of smoked or sea salt.

Assembly
1. Shake all ingredients together (except for powdered hemp) in a mixing tin with ice.
2. Strain and serve in a coupe.
3. Garnish with powdered hemp.

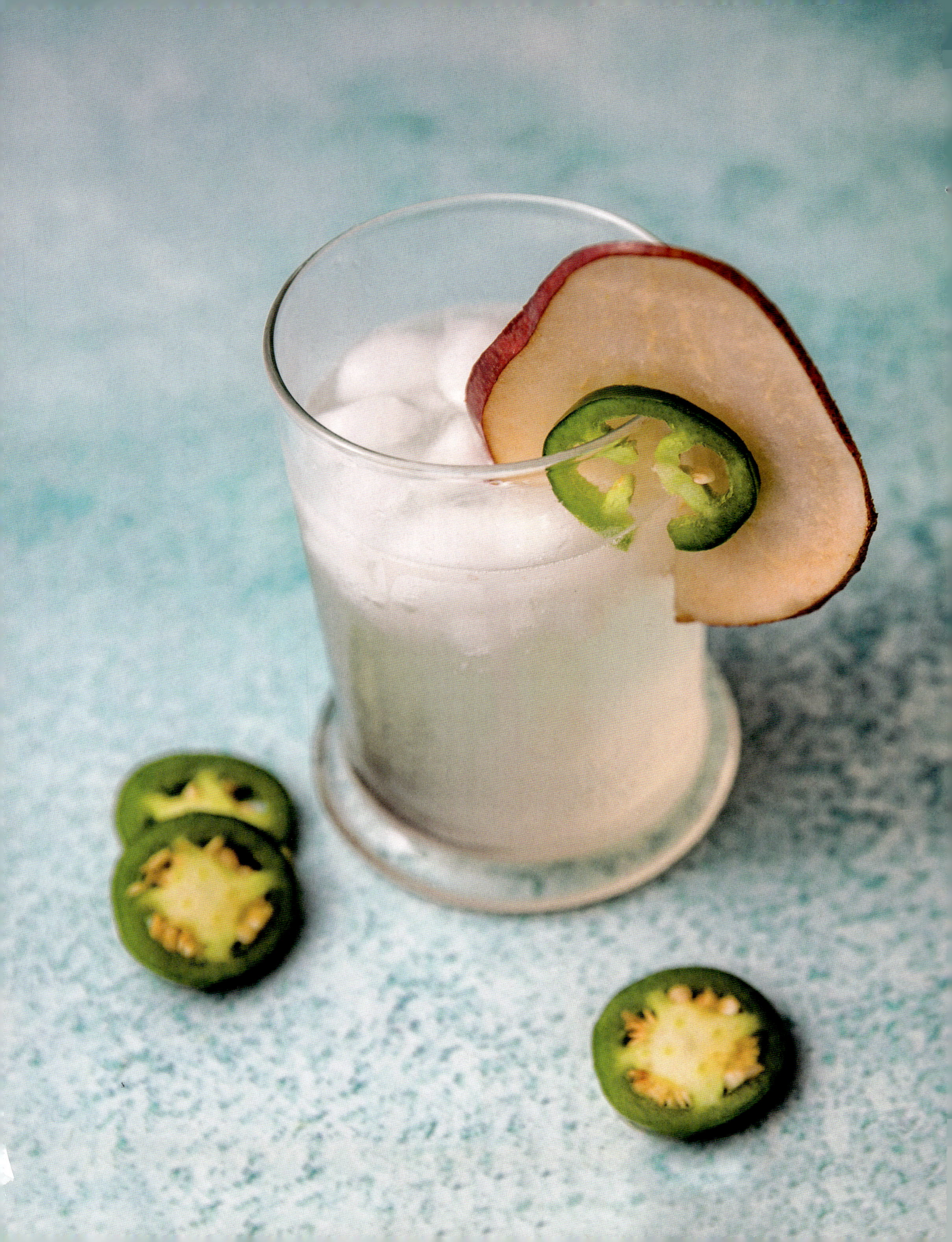

SERVING SIZE 2

DR. KANIKA TOMALIN'S BE PREPEARED

VODKA COCKTAIL WITH PROSECCO FLOATER

- 2 ounces pear-infused vodka
- 1 pear, thinly sliced
- 1 jalapeno, seeds removed and sliced
- Crushed ice
- Splash of prosecco
- 1 ounce pear nectar
- 1 tsp simply syrup

I mixed this sweet drink in memory of my sweetheart, my husband, Terry Tomalin, who passed away suddenly in 2016. Terry, longtime Outdoors Editor for the *Tampa Bay Times*, was a consummate outdoorsman who was always prepared. A Boy Scout leader and adventurer who traveled the world, he worked hard, played hard and always did as much as he could for others. After his passing, the hashtag **#TerryWouldGo** became a popular saying among the community of Terry's followers—a nod to his willingness to take on any challenge, and brave any adventure. For this low-calorie drink (make sure you use both a zero-calorie pear vodka and a low-calorie prosecco), I mix two of our favorites together: Terry's, vodka, and mine, prosecco. Infused with the light, crisp flavor of pear, with a little spice for a "pear-fectly" refreshing drink! **#TerryWouldGo**, and Terry would definitely dig this drink. I hope you do, too!

1. Combine pear nectar, 1 jalapeno slice, 1 pear slice, and vodka into a cocktail shaker filled with ice. Shake vigorously until chilled.
2. Wet the rim the glass with the juice of a pear slice; rim with sugar (optional).
3. Pour mixture over glass of crushed ice.
4. Add a floater of prosecco for sparkle; garnish with pear and jalapeno slices.

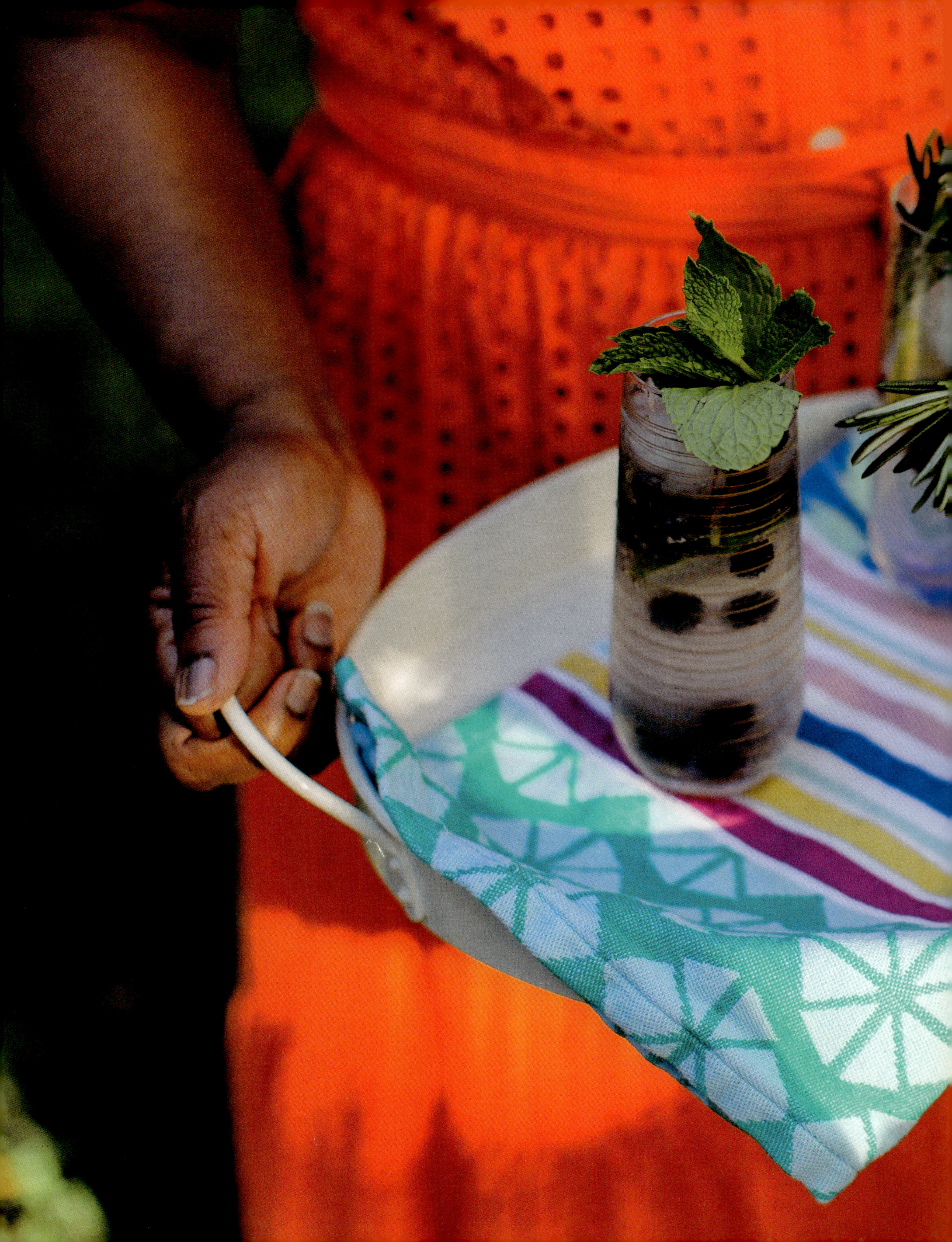

PARTICIPATING LOCATIONS

BellaBrava New World Trattoria, page 91, Pasta Arrabbiata
Brooklyn South, page 47, Mediterranean Tuna Salad
Callaloo, page 71, Southern Braised Callaloo Stew
Ceviche, page 33, Seafood Ceviche
Datz, page 63, Brie Bardot Sandwich
Dr. BBQ, page 59, Call Me Turkey
Ford's Garage St. Pete, page 115, The Aviator
Fresco's Waterfront Dining Bistro, page 87, Fresco Fish
Hawthorne Bottle Shoppe, page 51, Greens with a Kick
Ichicoro Ane, page 81, Mapo Tofu
Intermezzo, page 121, San Saba Songbird
Kahwa, page 109, Sugar-Free Sips
La V, page 29, Shrimp Spring Roll
Mandarin Hide, page 111, Matcha Made in Heaven
Noble Crust, page 85, Taste of Southern Italy
Pacific Counter, page 69, PC Kimchi
Paul's Landing, page 45, Power Bowl
Pipo's Cuban Cafe, page 99, Ropa Vieja
Punky's, page 67, Green Apple Cucumber Salad
Punky's, page 91, Veggie Lasagna
Red Mesa, page 53, Mango & Jicama Salad
Rococo Steak, page 31, Snapper Crudo
Rollin' Oats, page 83, Vegan Asparagus Risotto
Saigon Blonde, page 123, Hemp Day
Sea Salt, page 79, Dapper Snapper
TeBella Tea Company, page 117, Strawberry Mint Julep
The Birch & Vine, page 26, Szechuan Tuna & Bamboo Rice
The Canyon Cafe, page 100, Buddha Bowl
The Floribbean, page 88, Tropical Tails
The Left Bank Bistro, page 57, Nicoise Salad
The Library, page 61, Vegetarian Chili
The Library, page 97, Cauliflower Steak
The Library, page 119, Hemingway Daiquiri
The Lure, page 113, Thyme After Time
The Mill, page 43, Heirloom Watercress
The Tavern at Bayboro, page 49, The Adventurer Fresh Grouper
Trophy Fish, page 55, Best Dressed Catch
Urban Brew and BBQ, page 25, Everyday I'm Brusslin'

PHOTO CREDITS

Maria Flanagan: Front cover, back cover, pages 8-9, 11, 12-13, 14, 18-19, 20, 36, 38, 60, 68, 70, 92, 102, 104, 126-127.

James Ostrand Photography: pages 22, 24, 27, 28, 30, 32, 35, 40, 42, 44, 46, 48, 50, 53, 54, 56, 58, 62, 64, 66, 72, 74, 76, 78, 80, 82, 85, 86, 88, 90, 94, 96, 99, 100, 106, 110, 112, 114, 116, 118, 120, 122, 124.

City of St. Petersburg: pages 6, 7, 10, 16, 17.

Joey Clay: page 108.